On the Explanation of Chess and Backgammon

Abar Wizārišn ī Čatrang ud Nihišn Nēw-Ardaxšīr

On the Explanation of Chess and Backgammon

Abar Wizārišn ī Čatrang ud Nihišn Nēw-Ardaxšīr

Translated From Middle Persian by:
Touraj Daryaee

2016

Ancient Iran Series | Vol. 2

On the Explanation of Chess and Backgammon
Abar Wizārišn ī Čatrang ud Nihišn Nēw-Ardaxšīr

Cover: KB STUDI | Layout: KB STUDIO & SAM Arts Design Studio, LLC.
ISBN: 9781780836102

Printing by H&S Media © UK, 2016 | info@handsmedia.com

CONTENTS

To Nastaran Akhavan
for all her kindness

PREFACE

This book is the inaugural volume of the *Persian Text Series of Late Antiquity*, which aims at publishing most, if not all of the extant short Pahlavi texts in existence. There are several hundred Pahlavi and Pazand (Middle Persian written using the Avestan script) texts of various sizes in existence. These texts were committed to writing from the sixth century CE onward and are interesting in conveying late antique Iranian mores, values and beliefs. The Pahlavi texts are also part of the larger heritage of the Persian literature, which along with Pazand texts are the least studied and understood. It is hoped that the *Persian Text Series of Late Antiquity* contributes to the dissemination and study of these texts, which fill the gap between the Old Persian and Classical Persian literature.

The publication of this work is due to a generous grant from the *Roshan Cultural Heritage Institute* which supports *Sasanika: Late Antique Near East Project* at the Dr. Samuel M. Jordan Center for Persian Studies and Culture at University of California, Irvine. I would like to also thank the Afshar Publishing for agreeing to publish this work and the future Pahlavi and Pazand texts of the *Persian Text Series of Late*

Antiquity. I would like to thank my graduate student, Warren Soward for help in preparing the index glossary and my colleagues, Khodadad Rezakhani, Haleh Emrani and especially Yuhan S.-D. Vevaina and Arash Zeini for reading the manuscript and making constructive remarks.

Touraj Daryaee
Maseeh Chair in Persian Studies and Culture
Director of the Jordan Center for Persian Studies
University of California, Irvine

Introduction

Wizārišn ī Čatrang ud Nihišn Nēw-Ardaxšīr (henceforth *WČ*) is a Middle Persian text concerned with the earliest story of the invention of the games of chess and backgammon in the sixth century CE, during the rule of the great Sasanian king of kings, Khusro I (531-579 CE).[1] Four major personages play the part in this Middle Persian text, but only the Sasanian monarch has a firm historical attestation. These include the Indian king whose name is a matter of controversy and is read as Dēbšalm; his minister, Taxtrītos; and on the Persian side, Khusro I; and his famed Minister, Wuzurgmihr. A series of correspondences are exchanged between the Iranian and Indian court about which kingdom, its people and traditions, is loftier. As a measure of the intelligence of their people, the Indians devise a game (chess)

1. For the latest remarks on board games in the Iranian world, see U. Schädler and A.-E. Dunn-Vaturi, "Board Games in pre-Islamic Persia," *Encyclopaedia Iranica*, ed. E. Yarshater, 2009, http://iranica.com/articles/board-games-in-pre-islamic-persia.

and make a wager that the Iranians cannot figure out its logic. The Iranian sage, Wuzurgmihr not only unlocks the mystery of the game of chess, but also devises the game of backgammon (*Nēw-Ardaxšīr*) and sends it to the Indian court as a challenge. The Indian king along with Taxtrītos is unable to figure out the logic of the game and in this manner the Iranians achieve greatness over the Indians and continue to receive tribute. The story attempts to drive home several points to the audience. One is that not only the king of kings of the Sasanian Empire is greater than others, but also *Ērānšahr* (the name of the Sasanian Empire) is the greatest. Secondly, Wuzurgmihr is not only the greatest of the Persian sages, but greater than all the wise men in the world. He is also able to defeat the Indian sage three times in the game of chess which was invented by the Indians and creates a game whose logic the Indians cannot understand.

While Khusro I is well attested in the historical sources, Wuzurgmihr has received a good amount of study in regard to his historicity. Wuzurgmihr, the son of Bokhtag[2] is famous in Persian minister and sage who in is known as Buzurjmihr in

2.For all references regarding Wuzurgmihr, see Dj. Khaleghi-Motlagh, "Bozorgmehr-e Boḵtagān," *Encyclopaedia Iranica*, ed. E. Yarshater, 1989, http://iranica.com/articles/bozorgmehr-e-boktagan.

Persian literature.[3] His sayings make up not only part of the Middle Persian, but also Arabic wisdom literature. For example, there is the book entitled آداب بزرجمهر, preserved in the جاویدان خرد by Ibn Miskawayh,[4] where our sage remarks on the unreliability of the world, in line with our text, and also with Zoroastrian principals.[5] While the historicity of Wuzurgmihr's invention of the game of backgammon is unclear, the game of chess came from India and was part of the

---

3. In regard to his fictional nature and lack of historicity see Th. Nöldeke, "Burzōes Einleitung zum Buche Kalila we Dimna," *Schriften der Wissenschaft Ges. in Strassburg*, Vol. 12, 1912, p. 104f; for proponents of his historicity and his identification with Burzōe see, A. Christensen, "La légende du sage Buzurjmihr," *Acta Orientalia*, Vol. 8, 1929, pp. 81-127; For the influence of Khusro I and Wuzurgmihr in the post-Sasanian period see R.D. Marcotte, "Anushīrvān and Buzurgmihr - the Just Ruler and the Wise Counselor: Two figures of Persian Traditional Moral Literature," *Rocznik Orientalistyczny*, LI, 2, 1998, pp. 69-90.
4. Ibn Miskawayh, *Jāwīdān Khrad*, Kavoš Cultural Institute, Tehran, 1374, pp. 53-76.
5. M. Zakeri, *Persian Wisdom in Arab Garb. ʿAlī b. ʿUbayda al-Rayḥānī (D. 219/834) and his jawāir al-kilam wa-farāʾid al-ḥikam*, Brill, Leiden, Boston, 2007, P. 78. The opening sentence of Ādāb Buzurjmihr provides the fatalistic attitude which appears in our text: رأيت الدنيا ذات تصرف و زوال. Compare this with the Middle Persian text, *Ayādgār ī Wuzurgmihr ī Bōxtagān*, for which see Sh. Shaked, "Ayādgār ī Wuzurgmihr," *Encyclopaedia Iranica*, E. Yarshater, vol. 3, London, 1987, pp. 127-128.

great age of scientific and artistic transmission of knowledge to Iran from India during Late Antiquity.[6]

As for the Indian personages we are even less assured of their historicity. Ernst Herzfeld believed that the story of the invention of chess was transferred from Ardaxšīr I's time in the third century CE.[7] In fact this is inaccurate and it appears that not only the Ardaxšīr romance known as *The Deeds of Ardaxšīr, son of Pābag* (*Kārnāmag ī Ardaxšīr ī Pābagān*), but also such games originated in India and were brought during the reign of Khusro I. As mentioned the name of the Indian king is read variously as Dēbšalm, Dabšalm or Sačīdarmm, and in Persian and Arabic Dabšalim, which may be from

6. For a detailed study of the story of Wuzurgmihr and the transmission of knowledge from India to Iran see, F. de Blois, *Burzōy's Voyage to India and the Origin of the Book of Kalīlah wa Dimnah,* Royal Asiatic Society, London, 1990. A. Panaino has suggested that the game was in fact originally a game which existed in the West known as *ludus duodecim scriptorum, alea tabula*, Panaino, *La novella degli Scacchi e della Tavola Reale. Un'antica fonte orientale sui due gixochi da tavoliere piuà diffusi nel mondo euroasiatico tra Tardoantico e Medioevo e sulla loro simbologia militare e astrale. Testo pahlavi, traduzione e commento al Wizarišn î Chatrang ud nihišn î newardaxšîr "La spiegazione degli scacchi e la disposizione della tavola reale,"* Milano, 1999, p. 197.

7. E. Herzfeld, *Zoroaster and His World*, Vol. II, Octagon Books, New York, 1974, p. 628.

Sanskrit *Devaśarman* "God's joy," which appears in the *Hitopadeśa* "Book of Good Counsel."[8] De Blois has noted that as early as the 12th century CE, the Persian *Mujmal at-Tawārīkh wa l-Qiṣaṣ* mentions the game of chess and backgammon and the Indian king's name (*MTQ*):

> ازین پس شاه هندوان دابشلم شطرنج فرستاد و هزار خروار بار که اگر بازی به جا برنیارید همچنان زر و گوهر و ظرایفها که فرستاده بود بدهند. بزرجمهر آنرا بگشاد، و عوض آن نرد بساخت، و به هندوستان فرستاد، و همه حکماء هند جمع شدند، نتوانستند شناخت که آن بازی بر چه سانست، و بردانش او خستو شدند، و شطرنج بر مثال حرب ساختهاند، و آن قصه دراز است.[9]

> "Then Dābšalm, the king of the Indians sent chess and a thousand donkey load, that if you do not understand the game, the gold, jewels and goblets which he had sent be returned. Bozorgmihr

8. Th. Nöldeke, "Persische Studien," *Sitzungsberichte der K. Adademie der Wissenschaften in Wien*, Phil.-hist. Klasse, Vienna, Kl. 126, Abh. 12, 1892, pp. 21-23.
9. *Mujmal at-Tawārīkh wa l-Qiṣaṣ,* ed. M.-T. Bahār, Tehran, 1317, p. 75. The newly published facsimile of this text has داشليم which is of interest for our reading of the name, eds. M. Omidsalar & I. Afshar, Persian Manuscripts in Facsimile, No. 1, Tehran, 2001.

> unlocked (the logic of the game), and in return made backgammon and sent it to India and all the wise men of India gathered, (but) they could not figure in what manner the game is (played), and confessed to his knowledge, and they made the (game) of chess like battle and its story is long."

This passage is important for several reasons which we will come back to, but for now the name of the Indian king is given as Dābšalm which is close to C. Salemann's suggestion that in the *WČ* the name should be read as Dēbšalm (*dypšlm*).[10] The same doubt is also placed on the Indian wise man, Taxtrītos who sends to the Sasanian court 32 chess pieces made of emerald and red ruby to test the intelligence of the Iranians. When on the third day Wuzurgmihr rises and explains how the game must be played, he uses the analogy of the battle between two armies which appears in *Mujmal at-Tawārīkh wa l-Qiṣaṣ* in the likeness of war بر مثال حَرب.[11]

---

10. De Blois based on Salemann's suggestion emends the reading of the name to *dpšlm*, see C. Salemann, "Mittelpersische Studien. Erstes Stück," *Mélanges Asiatiques tirés de Bulletin de l'Académie impériale des sciences de St.-Pétersbourg IX*, 1887, p. 222; de Blois, p. 19.

11. *Mujmal at-Tawārīkh wa l-Qiṣaṣ* also supplies a short

What was the function of chess and backgammon as it appears in other Middle Persian sources in Sasanian Iran? Three other Middle Persian texts mention the game of chess and backgammon in a context that makes it clear that it was part of the princely or courtly education and in fact these texts themselves were part of what is called courtly literature.[12] In acquiring (Middle Persian) *frahang* > (Persian) فرهنگ which is equivalent to Greek *Paideia* and best can be translated as "culture," it appears that it was required that the nobility learn several arts including board games. These forms of knowledge were acquired in the *frahangestān* "education schools" for the nobility as there were *herbedestān* and *mowestān* the "priestly schools" established to train priests.[13] Thus, along with the physical training (jousting, polo, and the hunt), these games were part of the mental training of

---

version of the Middle Persian version, where Buzugmihr / Wuzurgmihr describes the game of chess to *ḥarb* "war," and the game of backgammon to *falak* "cosmos," ed. M-Š Bahār, Tehran, 1334, p. 75.

12. C.G. Cereti, *La letteratura Pahlavi, Introduzione ai testi con riferimenti alla storia degli studi e alla tradizione manoscritta*, Mimesis, Milano, 2001. pp. 191-192.

13. For a study of the requirements for king and princes in ancient Persia see W. Knauth, *Das altiranische Füerrstenideal von Xenephon bis Ferdousi*, nach d. antiken u. einheim. Quellen dargest, Franz Steiner, Wiesbaden, 1975.

the ancient Iranians. In this manner along with writing and memorization the Iranian world in Late Antiquity thus educated its elite.

The first Middle Persian text mentioning the game is named *Khusro ud Rēdag* "Khusro and the Page," which appears to take place at the court of king Khusro of our text.[14] The Page, who is from a noble line and whose parents have passed away, asks the king to look after him. In regard to his virtues, the Page states that he was most diligent in acquiring *frahang* while attending *frahangestān*. At the *frahangetān* his training included memorizing the sacred utterances, scribemanship, calligraphy, horsemanship, jousting, polo, playing musical instruments, singing, poetry, dancing, astronomical knowledge, and finally being master of the following board games (*Khusro ud Rēdag*, Jamasp-Asana 29.10-11):

> *ud čatrang ud nēw-ardaxšīr ud haštpāy kardan az hamahlān frāztar hēm*

---

14. D. Monchi-Zadeh, "Khusrov ī Kavātān ut Rētak, Pahlavi Text, Transcription and Translation," *Monumentum Georg Morgenstierne*, Vol. II, Acta Iranica 22, E.J. Brill, Leiden, 1982, pp. 47-91. For the best translation and work now see S. Azarnouche, *Husraw ī Kawādān ud Rēdag-ē/Khosrow fils de Kawād et un Page, texte pehlevi édité et traduit par* Samra Azarnouche, Studia Iranica, Cahier 49, Paris, 2013.

and in playing chess and backgammon
and haštpāy, I am ahead of (my) peers.[15]

Based on this text we can gain an insight into the conceptual view of acquiring culture in late antique Iran. Thus, *frahang* meant that a person who was to become a well-rounded person had to show not only prowess in physical training, but also sharpness of the mind. The second Middle Persian text where these games are mentioned is the *Kārnāmag ī Ardaxšīr ī Pābagān* (*The Book of the Deeds of Ardaxšīr, son of Pāpag*).[16] The text is about Ardaxšīr I's (224-240 CE) rise to power and his foundation of the Sasanian dynasty and the unification of *Ērānšahr*. The text, however, appears to be a late compilation

15. Pahlavi Texts, ed. Jamasp-Asana 29.10-11. Haštpay is from Sanskrit *aśṭāpada* < Persian *haštpāy* is similar to the chessboard and has 64 squares, 8 rows of 8 squares, H.J.R. Murray, *A History of Chess*, London, Oxford University Press, 1913, p. 33. The *Vinayapitaka*, a sacred Buddhist text from 4th or 3rd c. BC. introducing the *Dialogues of the Buddha*, enumerates a list of activities from which the converted man should keep remote. Among this list are games and among them are *aśṭāpada*, which means 8x8 gaming board, *http://history.chess.free.fr/ashtapada.htm*. For the latest study, see A. Panaino, "Haštpāy," *Encyclopaedia Iranica*, ed. E. Yarshater, 2003, http://www.iranica.com/articles/hastpay.
16. F. Grenet, *La Geste d'Ardashir fils de Pabag: Karnamag i Ardashir fils de Pdbagd*, Die, 2003, p. 60.

and its last redaction has been assigned to the seventh century CE., probably during the reign of Khusro II (590-628 CE).[17] In a part of the text where the virtues which made Ardaxšīr supersede other princes is discussed, the games of chess and backgammon are mentioned along with other sports as part of acquiring *frahang* (*Kārnāmag ī Ardaxšīr ī Pābagān* II.12):

> *pad yazdān ayyārīh pad čōbēgān ud aswārīh ud čatrang ud nēw-ardaxšīr ud abārīg frahang az awēšān hamōyēn čēr ud nibardag būd*
>
> "with the aid of the gods he (Ardaxšīr) was (more) victorious and experienced than all of them in polo and horsemanship and chess and backgammon and other *frahangs*."

The last Middle Persian text mentions the game of backgammon in a negative sense. In

17. O.M. Chukanova, *Kniga deianii Ardashira syna Papaka*, Pamiatniki Pis'mennosti Vostoka, Moscow, 1987, p. 162; the method used by Chukanova for dating the last redaction of the text has been criticized by A. Panaino, "The Two Astrological Reports of the Karnamag ī Ardaxšīr ī Pabagan (III, 4-7; IV,6-7)," *Die Sprache, Zeitschrift für Sprachwissenschaft*, Band 36, 1994, pp. 181-198.

the *Andarz ī Ošnar ī Dānāg* (*The Councils of the Wise Ošnar*), the path of moderation, (Middle Persian) *paymān* is emphasized,[18] where four things in excess are mentioned that lead to harm for mankind (*Andarz ī Ōšnar ī Dānāg* 33):

> *pad ēn 4 čiš rāy mard ziyānkārdar bawēd was xwardan ī may ud waranīg pad zanān ud was kardan ī nēw-ardaxšīr (ud) naxčīr nē pad paymānagīh*
>
> "With these four things man becomes more destructive: Drinking much wine, and lusting after women, and playing much backgammon, and hunting without moderation."[19]

Because of the late date of all these Middle

---

18. For the importance of moderation in the Iranian world see, Sh. Shaked, "Payman: an Iranian idea in contact with Greek thought and Islam," *Transition periods in Iranian history. Actes du Symposium de Fribourg-en-Brisgau (22-24 mai 1985)*, Studia Iranica. Cahier 5, Paris: Association pour l'Avancement des Etudes Iraniennes, 1987, pp. 217-240; and more recently, J. Amuzegar, "Paymān," *The Spirit of Wisdom [Mēnōg ī Xrad]. Essays in Memory of Ahmad Tafazzoli*, eds. T. Daryaee & M. Omidsalar, Mazda Publishers, Costa Mesa, 2004, pp. 32-42.
19. I.M. Nāzerī, *Andarz ī Ōšnar ī Dānā*, Hermand Publishers, Tehran, 1373, pp. 22-23.

Persian texts we can only state that by the time of Khusro I these games along with a variety of works were introduced to Iran from India. These include such texts as the *Pañcatantra* which according to tradition was translated into Middle Persian by the famous physician named Burzōe.[20] This Middle Persian work is unfortunately lost. However, a Syriac translation of it was made in CE 570 CE under the name of *Kalīlag wa Damnag*, this being the name of the two main players—"jackals"—in the Sanskrit text, *Karataka u Damanaka*. This story was also translated from Middle Persian into Arabic by 'Abdullāh ibn al-Muqaffa' in the eighth century CE, also known in Persian as the *Dāstānhāy-e Bidpāy* (*The Fables of Pilpay*). The Persian version of the *Dāstānhāy-e Bidpāy* which we have today is the version which was first translated from Sanskrit into Middle Persian and then to Arabic and then into Persian.[21] It was through this transmission of Sanskrit literature that the Buddhist *Jataka* stories came to Iran, later being translated into Greek, Latin, and Hebrew, which was to bring about the *Aesop's Fables* in

---

20. On Burzōe and the transmission of this type of literature to Iran, see de Blois, p. 53.
21. *Dāstānhāy-e Bīdpāy*, translated by Muḥammad b. Abdallāh al-Bukhārī, ed. P.N. Khānlarī and M. Roshan, Khārazmī Publishers, Tehran, 1369.

Byzantium, the *Sandbād-nāme*, and the *Arabian Nights*.[22]

These stories were taken from another Indian text called the *Hitopadeśa* (*Book of Good Counsel*). This book was part of the Indian genre known as *nitiśastra* "Mirror for Princes," which also existed in Iran, and in Middle Persian was known as *ēwēn-nāmag* > (Persian) آیین نامه "Book of Manners," which in the Middle Persian text on chess and backgammon is also mentioned to be part of this genre.[23] These books of manners or more commonly known as "Mirror for princes" is common in Arabic and Persian as well, being known as *Siyar al-muluk* or *Naṣiḥat al-muluk*. The reason why this body of texts was known as mirrors (Middle Persian *ēwēnag*) is best explained in *Dēnkard VI*:

> *awēšān ēn-iz ōwōn dāšt kū pad hammōzišn ī ōy ī did ān čišē ēn weh ka xēm ī xwēš be wirāyēd ud xwēštan ēwēnag be kunēd ud pēš ī ōy ī did dārēd ud ōy ī did andar nigerēd ud wēnēd ud az-iš abar hammōzēd*

22. A. Skilton, *A Concise History of Buddhism*, Barnes & Noble, New York, 1994, p. 200.
23. A. Tafazzolī, A. "Āʾīn-nāma," *Encyclopaedia of Iranica*, ed. E. Yarshater, Vol. 1, London, 1985, p. 692.

> "They held this too: In teaching one's fellow this one thing is best: That a man discipline his character, make a mirror of himself and hold it in front of his fellows. The other man looks at it, sees it and learns from it."[24]

The works which came from India were on such subjects as (Middle Persian) *tark* < (Sanskrit) *tarka* "logic," and (Middle Persian) *āwyākrn* < (Sanskrit) *vyākaraṇa* "rhetoric."[25] From the Greek world, works on (Middle Persian) *zamīg-paymānīh* "geometry," and Ptolemaios' (Middle Persian) *mgstyg* < μεγοτη' are known as well.[26] The transmission of scientific knowledge from India and Byzantium was current in the Sasanian period, especially works on astronomy and astrology to which the game of backgammon is related. The importance

---

24. Sh. Shaked, *The Wisdom of the Sasanian Sages*, Mazda Publishers, Costa Mesa, 1979, 223, pp. 86-87.
25. H.W. Bailey, *Zoroastrian Problems in the Ninth-Century Books*, Oxford, Clarendon Press, 1943; J. de Menasce, "Notes Iraniennes," *Journal Asiatique*, 1949, pp. 1-2; M. Boyce, "Middle Persian Literature," *Handbuch der Orientalistik, Iranistik*, Literatur, Lieferung 1, E.J. Brill, Leiden / Köln, 1968, pp. 36-37.
26. Bailey, *ibid.*, p. 86; Boyce, *ibid.*, pp. 36-37; For a review of all the material in Persian see H. Reza'ī Bāghbīdī, "Vāže Gozīnī dar As)r-e Sāsānī va Ta'sīr ān dar Fārsī-ye Darī," *Nāme-ye Farhangestān*, vol. 5, no.3, 1998 [2000], pp. 144-158.

which the Sasanians gave to these sciences is evident from a number of names which exist for the practitioners of these sciences.

The "astrologer" (Middle Persian) *axtarmār*; *starōšmār*, and "soothsayer" (Middle Persian) *murw-nīš*; *kēd*; *kundāg*, "zodiac-teller" (Middle Persian) *12-star-gōwišn*, "star-reckoner" (Middle Persian) *stārhangār*, and "time-knower" (Middle Persian) *hangām-šnās* were valued and active in this period which must have utilized and welcomed new Greek, Indian, and Babylonian astronomy and astrological material, and it appears that indeed the Sasanians brought about a mixture of the Greek, Indian, and Babylonian astrological material.[27]

According to the *Fihrist* of Ibn Nadim, the inventor of the game, Wuzurgmihr is also said to have written a commentary on the *Anthologiae* of Vettius Valens on astronomy which is lost, but fragments of the Arabic translation of the Middle Persian version exist.[28]

---

27. D. Pingree, "Astronomy and Astrology in India and Iran," *Isis, An International Review Devoted to the History of Science and its Cultural Influences*, Vol. 54, Part 2, No. 176, 1963, p. 241.

28. British Museum MS Add. 23,400, Pingree, *ibid.*, pp. 241-242; Brunner *op. cit.*, 1978, p. 46; Ibn Khaldūn gives similar information on Wuzurgmihr's preoccupation with astronomy and astrology, Pingree, *ibid.*, p. 245; that the Iranians were interested in astronomy already in the fifth century, before the influence of Indian material is indicated

The reason for discussing the preoccupation of Wuzurgmihr with astronomy and astrology is the cosmological explanation of the game of backgammon according to the Middle Persian text. This is different from the description of the function of the board game as we find it in the *Šāhnāmeh* of Ferdowsī. Wuzurgmihr's answer to the logic of the game of backgammon is central to Zoroastrian beliefs. The passage clearly demonstrates the cosmological significance of the game as described by Wuzurgmihr. His explanation is analogous to the processes of the cosmos and human life.[29] Wuzurgmihr makes fate the primary reason for what happens to mankind and the roll of the dice in the game performs the function of fate.[30] The pieces represent humans and their function in the universe is governed by the seven planets and the twelve zodiac signs. If we are to accept that Wuzurgmihr suggests "fate" (Middle Persian) *baxt* to be the

---

by E.S. Kennedy and B.L. van der Waerden, "The World-Year of the Persians," *Journal of the American Oriental Society*, Vol. 83, 1963, p. 323; Panaino believes that Wuzurgmihr is not the astrologer who translated the *Anthologiae*, Panaino, *La Novella*, p. 123.

29. Brunner, *op. cit.*, pp. 46-47.

30. C.J. Brunner, "Astrology and Astronomy II. Astronomy and Astrology in the Sasanian Period," *Encyclopaedia Iranica*, ed. E. Yarshater, Vol. II, Routledge & Kegan Paul, London and New York, 1987, p. 864.

principal determinant for one's life and action and take into consideration Eznik of Kołb's statement that in the Sasanian period, the deity Zurvān was equivalent to *baxt*, then we should (perhaps) consider Wuzurgmihr as a follower of the "Zurvanite" doctrine.[31] What is important is the difference between the game of chess and backgammon. While the game of chess is a game likened to battle, backgammon is based on the throw of the dice, thus based on one's fate.

According to some of the traditions of Zoroastrianism in the Sasanian period, fate dominated and controlled human life. The Middle Persian version of *Wīdēwdād* 5.9 (*Anti-Demonic Law*)[32] states:

> *gētīg pad baxt, mēnōg pad kunišn ast kē ēdōn gōwēd: zan ud frazand ud xwāstag ud xwadāyīh ud zīndagīh pad baxt,*

---

31. For a recent discussion of Zurvanism, see K. Rezania, *Die zoroastrische Zeitvorstellung. Eine Untersuchung über Zeit- und Ewigkeitskonzepte und die Frage des Zurvanismus* (Göttinger Orientforschungen, Iranica, N.F. 7), Wiesbaden, 2010.

32. For the Pahlavi text see, *The Zand î Javît Shêda Dât or the Pahlavi Version of the Avesta Vendidâd,* ed. D.P. Sanjana, Education Society Steam Press, Bombay, 1895, pp. 71-72. Most recently see, M. Moazami, *Wrestling with the Demons of the Pahlavi Widēwdād: Transcription, Translation, and Commentary*, E.J. Brill, 2014.

abārīg pad kunišn

The material world is (governed) through fate, the spiritual world is (governed) through action, there is somebody who says: wife and children and wealth and sovereignty and life is (governed) through fate, the rest is (governed) through action.

WČ as Compared with its Persian and Arabic Translations

The text was noteworthy enough to find Arabic and Persian prose and poetic renditions with differences. One should specifically pay attention to the *Šāhnāmeh* of Ferdowsī which contains the most detailed version of this text.[33] Tha'ālibī also has an abridged Arabic version of the story which is somewhat similar to the *Šāhnāme* and the Middle Persian version, but a bit longer than the *Mujmal at-Tawārīkh wa l-Qiṣaṣ*. The appearance of this story in the early Arabic and Persian texts suggests that it was part of the Sasanian *Xwadāy-nāmag* (*Book of Kings/Lords*) tradition which was translated by Ibn Muqafa' and transmitted for posterity. While Khusro I and Wuzurgmihr are

33. Š.H. Ghāsemī, "Peydāyeš-e Ṣatranj be Ravayat-e Šāhnāme," *Tahghighāt Islamī*, Vol. VI, 1991-1992, pp. 458-466.

mentioned in these texts, the name of the Indian king along with his minister are absent in Thaʿālibī and the *Šāhnāmeh*. It is only the *Mujmal at-Tawārīkh wa l-Qiṣaṣ* which supplies the name of the Indian king as Dabšalm. What is interesting is that the *Šāhnāmeh* provides the longest rendition of the story of chess and backgammon which has some very interesting details in terms of personages at the court of the Sasanian Empire. The story is such that the unnamed Indian king sends an envoy with 10 elephant loads of gold, silver, musk, ambergris and fresh-cut aloes wood, rubies, diamonds, Indian swords, and whatever is produced in Kannuj with a letter (*ŠN* 2676-2678):[34]

فراوان به بار اندرون سیم و زر   چه از مشک و عنبر، چه از عود تر
ز یاقوت و الماس و از تیغ هند   همه تیغ هندی سراسر پرند
زچیزی که خیزد ز قنوج و رای   زده دست و پای، آوریده به جای

Here the story follows that of the *WČ*, where the Indian king mentions that they will continue to pay tribute if the Iranians figure out the logic

34. Dj. Khaleghi-Motlagh & A. Khatibi, *The Shahnameh (The Book of Kings)*, Bibliotheca Persica, New York, Vol. 7, 2007, pp. 304-319; The English prose translation of this section is also available, see D. Davis, *Shahnameh. The Persian Book of Kings*, A New Translation by Dick Davis, Viking, New York, 2006, p. 699.

of the game, but if not, they will stop doing so. Another difference here is that the Indian king mentions the different pieces of the game before hand and the Indian messenger tells Khusro that the logic of the game of chess is like warfare (*ŠN* 2697):

چنین داد پاسخ که ای شهریار همه رسم و راه ازدر کارزار

Khusro asks for a week to figure out the game, whereas in the *WČ* there is no limit set. Here Wuzurgmihr (Bozorgmihr in the *ŠN*) studies the game for one day and night and then comes before the Iranian king to explain its logic, while in the *WČ* Wuzurgmihr stands up on the third day and explains the game of chess. The Indian messenger is dumbfounded and the Iranians are overjoyed. As a reward Khusro gives Wuzurgmihr a goblet filled with jewels (*ŠN* 2747):

یکی جام فرمود پس شهریار که کردند پر گوهر شاهوار

I believe the mention of the goblet is important for another reason and aids in the decipherment of the Middle Persian text. Here the story diverges and the *ŠN* becomes detailed and interesting for some of its historical facts and traditions which may aid us in understanding the identity of the Indian king and his kingdom.

Wuzurgmihr devises the game of backgammon and Khusro sends him to India along with two thousand camels loaded with goods from Rome, China, Hephthalite, Makran and the Iranian realm (*ŠN* 2768):

زباری که خیزد ز روم و زچین   ز هیتال و مکران و ایران زمین

Here, the limits of the Indian king's realm is mentioned by Khusro which may give us an idea about the identity of the king. Khusro in his letter mentions the realm of the Indian king from the Sea or Lake of Kannuj to Sind (*ŠN* 2774):

دگر گفت کای نامور شاه هند   ز دریای قنوج تا پیش سند

If we are to take this geographical reference to an Indian king and kingdoms of the period we come across a few possible locations, where the most important king is Yaśōdharma. In fact J. Markwart and de Groot associated our Indian king Dēbšalm with king Yaśōdharma who was the contemporary of Khusro I in the sixth century CE. Marquart's idea was that *dypšlm* was a corruption of Middle Persian *yswdhlm* / Yaśōdharma.[35] Yaśōdharma was able to carve out

35. J. Markwart and de Groot, J.J.M. "Das Reich Zābul und der Gott Zūn," *Eduard Sachau-Festschrift*, 1915, p. 257.

an empire for himself after defeating the Huns in the sixth century. His kingdom bordered the Gupta Empire, which fell into anarchy by the mid sixth century CE. It is thought that it was during the Gupta period that the game of chess, or its original form came about along with a host of other scientific matters, including astronomy, mathematics, wisdom literature and medicinal texts. Also, it is the Gupta Empire which expanded from Kannuj to Sind. This is important in that Khusro I and the Sasanians sought knowledge from India, specifically sciences related to medicine,[36] and so the Gupta Empire appears to be important. Thus, conflation of a heroic and famous Indian king along with a fabled kingdom of India may be behind our Iranian tradition of both the *WČ* and the *Šāhnāmeh*.

Going back to the *Šāhnāmeh*, Wuzurgmihr is sent with the caravan and the letter to the Indian court. The Indian sages, however, are unable to solve the logic of the game of backgammon which in the *ŠN* is again likened to the game of chess, resembling warfare. This is a notable difference from our *WČ* which explains the game very differently, based on cosmological

36. De Blois suggests that the real goal of the Sasanians from the mission of Burzōe, who is the famous Iranian doctor, was to gain information on medicine, p. 64.

speculation. In the *ŠN* the Indian king gives more tribute to be sent back to *Ērānšahr* and a letter stating that Khusro is the exceptional ruler of all times. Thus, the *Šāhnāmeh* serves best as a parallel literary text to that of the *WČ* which is even a longer exposition of the story that was circulating in Eurasia, while Tha'ālibī and *Mujmal at-Tawārīkh wa l-Qiṣaṣ* tend to give brief, but interesting details supporting the story of the *WČ*.

Chess and Backgammon in Art and Material Culture

The earliest existing material culture in reference to chess from the Iranian world is an elephant carved from black stone, dated to the late sixth or seventh century CE, which corresponds to the approximate time when the *WČ* was composed.[37] There is also a silver-gilded hemispherical bowl dated to the seventh century CE,[38] which depicts several important scenes from the Sasanian period. These include a marriage ceremony, a wrestling contest, and several other episodes including a

---

37. E. Herzfeld, "Ein Sasanidischer Elefant," *Archäologische Mitteilungen aus Iran*, Vol. III, 1931, p. 27; C.K. Wilkinson, *Chess: East and West, Past and Present, A Selection from the Gustavus A. Pfeiffer Collection*, The Metropolitan Museum of Art, New York, 1968, xxxvii.
38. A. C. Gunter and P. Jett, *Ancient Iranian Metalwork in the Arthur M. Sackler Gallery and the Freer Gallery of Art*, Smithsonian Institution, Washington, D.C., 1992, p. 163.

scene of two people playing backgammon. One can suggest that this bowl represents the things that mattered in courtly life,[39] and that the scenes on the bowl represent the activities which a noble should engage in. Another early pictorial portrayal of the game of backgammon comes from Central Asia, from the city of Panjikent, in modern Tajikistan.

These paintings show religious, as well as heroic and epic, scenes. Some of the paintings depict such epic stories as that of Rustam's battles, the mourning for Siyāwaxš (Persian) *sōg ī siyāwaš* and other imagery known in the Iranian world.[40] The

39. P.O. Harper, *The Royal Hunter, Art of the Sasanian Empire*, The Asia Society, New York, 1978, p. 75.
40. G. Azarpay, *Sogdian Painting, The Pictoral Epic in*

painting in question shows two people playing a board game which in all probability is a backgammon game along with several other personages beside them. The exact context of the story is not clear, but it has been suggested that the scene either represents a Buddhist Jātaka story or a Turco-Iranian narrative theme.[41] A nimbus appears to encircle the head of one of the players who has his right hand raised as a gesture of victory. The man seated on the left again has his left hand raised showing the bent forefinger. A figure behind the victorious person also appears to be pointing to the loser with the bent forefinger. The bent forefinger here demonstrates one's submission or defeat at the game, confirmed through the acknowledgment of another person with the same gesture as witness.[42]

Directly related to *WČ* is a fourteenth century illuminated manuscript of the *Šāhnāme* which contains two scenes, one at the court of Khusro I, and the second at the court of Dēbšalm. In the scene Wuzurgmihr is seated on the floor with

---

Oriental Art, University of California Press, Berkeley, Los Angeles and London, 1981.

41. M. Bussagli, *Painting of Central Asia*, The World Publishing Company, Ohio, 1963, pp. 46-47.

42. J.K. Choksy, "Gesture in Ancient Iran and Central Asia II: Proskynesis and the Bent Forefinger," *Bulletin of the Asia Institute*, Vol. 4, 1990[1992], p. 205.

three other Persians all with white turbans. In front of the Persian sage is a board game, which by taking into account the story, we can deduce to be a backgammon board. The Indian king is seated on his throne and is surrounded by the Indian sages who are painted darker and have darker turbans. Wuzurgmihr has his right hand pointing to the backgammon board, which probably means that he is either challenging the Indian sages or explaining the rules of the game after the Indian sages are left staggered. It is particularly interesting to note that one of the two older Indian sages who have a white beard has his hand over his mouth, symbolizing his amazement. We should also note that the design of the board is very similar to that of the board on the wall paintings at Panjikent.[43]

43. C.K. Wilkinson, p. xii.

The Game of Chess and Backgammon beyond Sasanian Iran

According to Tha'ālibī, when the Arab Muslims conquered the Sasanian capital of Ctesiphon in the seventh century CE, they found a set of backgammon pieces belonging to Khusro II, which were made of coral and turquoise. This, however, was not the first encounter of the Arabs with such board games. As early as the time of the Prophet Muhammad, the game of backgammon had already made its way from Iran to Arabia.[44] These games in fact became popular in the Islamic world, where they were played by the masses and the nobility alike. During the early Abbāsīd period the game of backgammon was popular both at the court of Hārūn al-Rashid and that of his son, al-Ma'mūn. It is said that al-Ma'mūn liked to play

44. F. Rosenthal, *Gambling in Islam*, E.J. Brill, Leiden, 1975, p. 88.

backgammon since, if he lost, he could place the blame on the dice, meaning fate.[45] Medieval authors justified the game of chess by stating that as long as it was played for mental exercise it would be beneficial. The eleventh century Persian treatise by Kaykawus ibn Iskandar entitled *Qābūsnāme* dedicates a chapter to the games of Chess and Backgammon, where he comments upon the proper etiquette of playing, as well as when and to whom one should lose or win from. It is strictly stated that one should not make bets on the games and only then playing the game becomes a proper activity.[46] From the Seljuk period, it is reported that Alp Arslan was also fond of backgammon and throwing double sixes with the dice.[47]

It is this Iranian form of the game that spread

---

45. Murry, *op. cit.,* p. 115.

46. 'Unsur al-ma'ālī Kai-Kāwūs b. Iskadar b. Qabūs b. Wašmgīr b. Ziyār, *Qābūsnāme*, ed. Q.-H. Yusefī, Scientific and Cultural Publishers, Tehran, 1375, p. 77.

47. It is said that he once became angry when he had one six rather than a double six, see Ahmad b. 'Umar b. 'Alī Nizāmī Arūzi Samarghandī, *Čahār maghāle*, ed. M. Ghazvini and M. Mo'īn, Armaghān Publishers, Tehran, 1331, pp. 68-69; certain manuscripts mention *se* "three" instead of *do* "two" for the number of dice. Qazvini's manuscript has two, but there is also evidence of the game being played with three dice. In *Nafāyis al-fun,n fi 'arāyis al-'uyūn*, by Muhammad b. Mahmūd Āmolī, ed. Mirza Ahmad, Tehran, 1309, Vol. II, p. 220, regarding the game of backgammon, three dice are mentioned and again the game is likened to the cosmos.

to the rest of the Near East and Anatolia. Today when playing the game in Turkey and in the Arab countries, the game is called *shesh-baish*, *nard* or *nardi* or (Arabic) *tāwula*. The technical terminology generally used is in Persian. For example numbers: *yuk* < Persian *yak* < Middle Persian *ēk*; *du* < Persian *do* < Middle Persian *dō*; *sey* < Persian *se* < Middle Persian *sē*; *jahr* < Persian *čāhār* < Middle Persian *čahār*; *benj* < Persian *panj* < Middle Persian *panj*; and *shesh* < Persian *šeš* < Middle Persian *šaš*. When calling combinations, they are rarely called out in either Arabic or Persian, for example *shesh-baish* or *dū-yuk*.[48] In Georgia the game is called *nardi*, and in Central Asia it is called *narr*; in the Deccan the game is called *tukhta-e-nard* from Persian *takht-e nard*.[49]

The most important work in the medieval Christian world on this subject is entitled *Libro de los juegos* (*Book of Games*), commissioned by king Alfonso X of Castile in the thirteenth century CE to translate the rules of chess and backgammon from Arabic into Latin.[50] But it seems that the

---

48. R. A. Barakat, *Tāwula: A Study in Arabic Folklore*, Suomalainen Tiedeakatemia, Academia Scientiarum Fennica, Helsinki, 1974, pp. 10-11.
49. Murray, H. J. R. *A History of Chess*, London, Oxford University Press, 1913.p. 115.
50. J.O. Dramiga, *Eine kurze Kulturgeschichte des Schachspiels*, http://www.schachbund.de/downloads/Kulturgeschichte-des-Schachs.pdf, 2009, p. 10.

game had reached Spain (Córdoba) in 822 CE, apparently by a talented Iranian Muslim from Baghdad named Abu l-Hasan 'Ali ibn Nafi', known as Ziryab (in Persian *Zaryāb* meaning "wealth/gold finder").[51] It is from Spain that the game traveled to most of the European world. By the time the Spaniards were able to push out the Muslims from Andalusia, one piece of the game was also changed. In the fifteenth century the Spanish text entitled *Libre dels jochs partits dels schachs en nombre de 100* (*The Book of 100 Chess Problems*), published in Valencia (1495 CE) by Francesch Vicent, the queen and her enhanced position is discussed.[52] Thus, the queen replaced the *Vazīr,* and in this way, the game was influenced by the Spanish tradition as well. The Spanish brought the game of chess to America where it became a favorite game for intellectuals and men of politics. In 1779, Benjamin Franklin wrote a famous essay entitled "On the Morals of Chess," where he acknowledged the antiquity of the game in such a manner: "Playing at Chess is the most ancient and most universal game among men; for its origin is beyond the memory of history, and it has, for numberless ages, been the amusement of all the civilized

51. M. Yalom, *Birth of the Chess Queen. A History*, Harper Collins Publishers, New York, 2004, P. 11.
52. Yalom, P. 195.

nations of Asia, the Persians, the Indians, and the Chinese."[53] But what is important is that Franklin states that playing chess teaches one foresight, circumspection and caution,[54] which is in line with the twelve hundred year old Persian version of *WČ*. Thus, from Sasanian Iran these games made their way around the world and became popular and well-known in Europe and America. Benjamin Franklin did not know of *WČ*, but it is now presented here as the first story of invention, and the manual of the rules of the games of chess and backgammon in the world.

---

53. B. Franklin, "On the Morals of Chess," reprinted in *The Chess Player, Illustrated with Engravings and Diagrams. Containing, Franklin's Essay on the Morals of Chess, Introduction to the Rudiments of Chess, by George Walker, Teacher, to which are added, The Three Games played at one and the same time by Philidor, Sixty Openings, Mates and Situations, by W.S. Kenny, Teacher, with Remarks, Anecdotes, and an Eplanation of the Round Chess Board,* Published by Nathl. Dearborn, Boston, 1841, pp. 7-11.
54. Franklin, P. 8.

Previous Study of the Text

The text has been the subject of several studies in the nineteenth and the twentieth centuries.[55] These include the first translation into English in 1885 by the Parsi scholar, D.P.B. Sanjana,[56] and two years later into German by C. Salemann.[57] In the twentieth century it was J.C.

55. For all studies pertaining to the text and its translation see C.G. Cereti, *La Letteratura Pahlavi, Introduzione ai testi con riferimenti alla storia degli studi e alla tradizione manoscritta*, Mimesis, Milano, 2001, pp. 203-205.

56. D.P.B. Sanjana, *Ganje shâyagân andarze Atrepât Mârâspandân, Mâdigâne chatrang and Andarze Khusroe Kavâtân. The Original Péhlvi Text, the same Transliterated in Zend Characters and Translated into the Gujrati and English Languages, a Commentary and a Glossary of Selected Words*, Bombay, 1885.

57. C. Salemann, Mittelpersische Studien. Ersets Stük (*sic*). *Mélanges Asiatiques tirés du Bulletin de l'Académie Impériale des Sciences de St. Pétersbourg*, Tome IX, Livraison 3, 1887, pp. 222-242.

Tarapore[58] who provided the first English translation, followed by two Italian scholars M. Lucidi[59] and A. Pagliaro,[60] and in Russian by I.A. Orbeli and K. Trever.[61] In the second half of the twentieth century C.J. Brunner,[62] and A. Panaino[63] provided translations of the text based on the edition of JamaspAsana which used the important MK manuscript.[64] Others have also provided corrections and notes to the text which have improved our readings of certain words. One should mention H.S. Nyberg whose notes to the

58. J.C. Tarapore, *Vijārishn-i chatrang or the Explanation of Chatrang and other Texts, Transliteration and translation into English and Gujarati. The Original Pahlevi Texts. With an Introduction*, Bombay, 1932.
59. M. Lucidi, *Il Testo Pahlavico Vičārišni čatrang ud nihišni nēw-artaxšēr*, Scuola Orientale, Universita di Roma, 1935-1936.
60. A. Pagliaro, *Il Testo Pahlavico Sul Giuoco degli Scacchi*, in Miscellanea G. Galbiati, Vol. III, Fontes Ambrosiani VIII, Milano, 1951, pp. 97-110.
61. I.A. Orbeli and K. Trever, *Šarang. Kniga o šahmatah*, Leningrad, 1936.
62. C.J. Brunner, "The Middle Persian Explanation of Chess and Invention of Backgammon," *The Journal of the Ancient Near Eastern Society of Columbia University*, Vol. 10, 1978, pp. 43-51.
63. A. Panaino, *La Novella degli Scacchi e della Tavola Reale*, Mimesis, Milano, 1999.
64. J.M. Jamasp-Asana, *The Pahlavi Texts Contained in the Codex MK copied in 1322 A.C. by the Scribe Mehr-Âwân Kaí-khûsrû*, Fort Printing Press, Bombay, 1913.

original Pahlavi text and his dictionary made significant improvements in our knowledge.[65] E.W. West,[66] O. Hansen,[67] and A. Cantera[68] have also made important comments in previous works. There have been three Persian translations of the text, that of M.T. Bahār,[69] followed by S. Oriān,[70] and finally the best Persian translation and edition by B. Gheiby.[71] A. Panaino has done the most detailed study of the *WČ* in Italian, along with commentary and index which is used in this work.

---

65. H.S. Nyberg, *A Manual of Pahlavi*, Otto Harrassowitz, Wiesbaden, 1964, pp. 118-121.
66. E.W. West, "Note on the Catrang-namak," *Journal of the Royal Asiatic Society*, 1898, pp. 389-390.
67. O. Hansen, *Zum mittelpersichen Vičārišn čatrang*, Internationalen Orientalistenkongress in rom, Verlag J.J. Augustinus in Glückstadt Holst, 1935, pp. 13-19.
68. A. Cantera, Review of A. Panaino's *La Novella degli Scacchi e della Tavola Reale* in *Orientalistiche Literaturzeitung*, vol. 95, no. 3, 2000, pp. 304-311.
69. M.T. Bahār, "Gozāresh-e šatrang va nahādan-e vanirdšēr," *Tarjumeh-ye čand matn-e pahlavī*, Tehran, 1347, pp. 10-17.
70. S. Oriān, *Motūn-e pahlavī*, National Library of Iran, Tehran, 1371, pp. 152-157, 226-342.
71. B. Gheiby, *Guzāreš-e Šatranj*, Nemudar Publications, Bielefeld, 2001.

The Manuscripts

The MK codex which contains the *Wizārišn ī Čatrang ud Nihišn ī Nēw-Ardaxšīr* was used by K.J. Jamasp-Asana for his edition of the text. The codex consisted of 163 folios where the *Wizārišn ī Čatrang ud Nihišn ī Nēw-Ardaxšīr,* along with a variety of texts, some short and a few longer ones, such as *the Ayādgār ī Zarērān*, and *Husraw ud Rēdag* appear. However, this manuscript was missing until it was recently found and is to be published by A. Hintze and K.M. Jamasp-Asa.[72] The text appears on eight folios, each containing nineteen to twenty one lines. This part of the manuscript is withered and part of each page is missing. It was solely due to the kindness of A. Hintze that I was able to have access to the

72. K.M. JamaspAsa and A. Hintze, *The Pahlavi codex MK. Facsimile and Introduction.* Otto Harrassowitz, Wiesbaden, Iranica 20 (forthcoming 2012).

manuscript which contains the surviving portion of the text. This manuscript allows us to see the oldest manuscript available to us for the WČ.

Also of interest is the neglected MU2 manuscript published by the Asia Institute of Shiraz University.[73] MU2 was originally housed at the K.R. Cama Oriental Institute in Mumbai. The manuscript contains 13 different texts and has no colophon. The codex consists of 161 folios, each containing eleven lines. The *Wizārišn ī Čatrang ud Nihišn ī Nēw-Ardaxšīr* is found in fol. 138 - fol. 150 and is reproduced here. This manuscript appears to be inferior to MK and others.

What I have called the J Manuscript is in fact Jamasp-Asana's edition which is the basis of most works done on *WČ*, including this edition which used three manuscripts: TD, MK and JJ. The *WČ* is part of this edition found in fol. 115 - fol. 120.[74] What I call the S manuscript is the edition by Peshutan Dastur Behramji Sanjana[75]

---

73. *The Pahlavi Codices and Iranian Researches: Manuscript MU2*, eds. Kh.M. Jamasp Asa & M. Navabi, Published by the Asia Institute of Pahlavi University, no. 35, Shiraz, 1976.

74. Jamasp-Asana, *The Pahlavi Texts Contained in the Codex MK copied in 1322 A.C. by the Scribe Mehr-Âwân Kaí-khûsrû*, Fort Printing Press, Bombay, 1913.

75. Sanjana, D.P.B. *Ganje shâyagân andarze Atrepât Mârâspandân, Mâdigâne chatrang and Andarze Khusroe*

who used three manuscripts, the oldest by an unknown priest at Broach for the use of his student, named Farrokh Hormazd. The second manuscript is a copy of the above-mentioned manuscript by Dastur Rustamjee Behramji Sanjana, dated to 1131 Yazdgerdi at Surat. The third copy is another copy of the second copy. Indeed this edition by Jamasp-Asana is very good and useful for editing the *WČ*.

Kavâtân. The Original Péhlvi Text, the same Transliterated in Zend Characters and Translated into the Gujrati and English Languages, a Commentary and a Glossary of Selected Words, Bombay, 1885.

Transcription

pad nām ī yazdān

1) ēdōn gōwēnd kū andar xwadāyīh ī husraw anōšag-ruwān az dēbšalm ī wuzurg šahryār ī hindūgān šāh abar uzmūdan ī xrad ud dānāgīh ī ērān[76]-šahrīgān[77] ud sūd-īz ī xwēš nigerīdan rāy čatrang ēw juxt 16 tāg az uzumburd ud 16 tāg az yākand ī suxr kard frēstīd[78]. 2) abāg ān čatrang 1000 ud 200 uštar bār zarr ud asēm ud gōhr ud morwārīd ud jām[79] <ud> 90 pīl u-š čiš ī mādagīg kard abāg frēstīd[80] ud tāxtarītos čiyōn andar[81] hindūgān pad wizēn[82] būd abāg frēstīd. 3) pad

76. MU 'yl'n + otiose stroke
77. MK štl'
78. MU ŠDRWN-nd
79. JA, MU, S = y'm'k
80. MU ŠDRWN-nd
81. MU omits
82. MK yyw'

frawardag[83] ōwōn nibišt ēstād kū abāyēd čiyōn ašmā nām pad šāhān-šāhīh pad amā hamāg šāhān-šāh hēd abāyēd kū dānāgān ī ašmā az ān ī amā[84] dānāgtar bawēnd agar čim ī ēn čatrang wizārēd ēnyā sāk ud bāj frēstēd. 4) šāhān-šāh 3 rōz zamān xwāst ud ēč kas nē būd az dānāgān ī ērānšahr kē čim ī ān čatrang wizārdan šāyēst. 5) sidīgar rōz wuzurgmihr ī bōxtagān abar ō pāy ēstād[85]. 6) u-š guft kū anōšag bawēd[86] man čim ī ēn čatrang tā im rōz[87] az ān čim[88] rāy be nē wizārd tā ašmā ud harw kē pad ērānšahr hēd[89] be dānēd kū[90] andar ērānšahr mard ī man dānāgtar hom. 7) man čim ī ēn čatrang xwārīhā wizārom ud sāk ud bāj az[91] dēbšalm stānom ud anē-iz čiš-ēw kunom ō dēbšalm frēstom ī-š wizārdan nē tuwān az-iš <ud> 2[92] bārag sāk ud bāj[93] man gīrom ud pad ēn abēgumān bawēd kū ašmā pad šāhān-šāhīh arzānīg hēd ud dānāgān ī amā az ān ī dēbšalm dānāgtar hēnd. 8) šāhān-

83. MU plwlt
84. MK repeated twice
85. MK YKOYMWN-yt
86. MU YHWWN-'t
87. MU omits
88. MK omits
89. MK omits
90. MU and MK = AMT
91. MK omits
92. MK omits
93. JA and MU omits

šāh 3 bār guft kū zīwā wuzurgmihr tātarītos ī amā u-š 12000[94] drahm ō wuzurgmihr framūd dādan. 9) rōz ī dudīgar wuzurgmihr tātarītos ō pēš xwāst ud guft kū dēbšalm ēn čatrang pad čim ī kārezār homānāg kard. 10) u-š homānāg 2 sar-xwadāy kard šāh ō mādayārān raxw ō hōyag ud dašnag ō homānāg frazēn ō artēštārān-sālār homānāg [pīl ō puštībānān-sālār homānāg ud asb ō][95] aswārān-sālār homānāg payādag ō ān ham-payādag homānāg ī pēš-razm. 11) u-š pas tātarītos čatrang nihād ud abāg wuzurgmihr wāzīd[96] ud wuzurgmihr[97] 3 dast az tātarītos burd ud padiš wuzurg rāmišn ō hamāg kišwar mad. 12) pas tātarītos abar ō pāy ēstād[98]. 13) u-š guft kū anōšag bawēd yazad ēn warz ud xwarrah ud amāwandīh ud pērōzgarīh ō ašmā dād ērān ud anērān xwadāy hēd. 14) čand tā dānāgān ī hindūgān ēn čatrang ēw juxt nihād pad was harg ud ranj[99] ō ēd gyāg āwurd ud ēč kas wizārdan nē tuwān būd. 15) wuzurgmihr ī ašmā az āsnxrad ī xwēš ēdōn xwārīhā ud sabukīhā be wizārd. 16) u-š ān and xwāstag ō ganj ī šāhān-šāh wisē

94. MU 10 + 1000

95. JA and MU missing [pīl ō puštībānān-sālār homānāg ud asb ō]

96. MK omits

97. MK omits

98. MU YKOYMWN-yt

99. MK YWM

kard. 17) šāhān-šāh dudīgar rōz wuzurgmihr ō pēš xwāst.18) u-š ō wuzurgmihr guft kū wuzurgmihr[100] ī amā čē ast ān čiš ī-t guft kū kunom ō dēbšalm frēstom. 19) wuzurgmihr guft kū az dahibedān[101] andar ēn hazārag[102] ardaxšīr kardārtar ud dānāgtar būd ud nēw-ardaxšīr ēd juxt pad nām ī ardaxšīr nihom. 20) taxtag ī nēw-ardaxšīr ō spandarmad zamīg homānāg kunom. 21) ud 30 muhrag ō 30 rōz ud šabān homānāg kunom 15 spēd ō rōz homānāg kunom ud 15 syā ō šab homānāg kunom. 22) gardānāg ēw-tāg ō wardišn ī axtarān ud gardišn ī spihr homānāg kunom. 23) ēk abar gardānag-ēw[103] ōwōn homānāg kunom kū ohrmazd ēk ast ud har nēkīh ōy dād. 24) 2 ēdōn homānāg kunom čiyōn mēnōg ud gētīg. 25) 3 ōwōn homānāg kunom čiyōn humat ud hūxt ud huwaršt ud menišn ud gōwišn ud kunišn. 26) 4 ōwōn homānāg kunom čiyōn čahār āmēzišn kē mardōm az-iš u-š čahār sōg ī gētīg xwarāsān ud xwarwarān ud nēmrōz ud abāxtar. 27) 5 ōwōn[104] homānāg kunom čiyōn 5[105] rōšnīh čiyōn xwaršēd ud māh ud stārag ud

100. MU pwl Y mtr'
101. MU & S followed by Y
102. MK hc'l
103. S glt'n'k'
104. MK missing
105. MK missing

ātaxš ud warzag az asmān āyēd[106]. 28) 6 ōwōn homānāg kunom čiyōn dādan ī dām pad 6 gāh ī gāhānbār. 29) nihādag ī nēw-ardaxšīr abar taxtag ēdōn homānāg kunom čiyōn ohrmazd xwadāy ka-š dām ō gētīg dād. 30) wardišn ud gardišn ī muhrag pad gardānāg-ēw ōwōn homānāg kunom[107] čiyōn mardōmān ī andar gētīg band ō mēnōgān paywast ēstēd pad 7 ud 12 hamāg wardēnd ud wihēzēnd ud ka ast ēk ō did zanēnd ud abar čīnēnd čiyōn mardōmān andar gētīg ēk ō did zanēnd. 31) ud ka pad gardānāg-ē ēd gardišn hamāg abar čīnēnd hangōšīdag ī mardōm[108] kē [hamāg az gētīg widārān bawēnd ud ka did-iz be nihēnd hangōšīdag ī mardōmān][109] kē pad ristāxēz hamāg zīndag abāz bawēnd. 32) šāhān-šāh ka-š[110] ān saxwan āšnūd rāmišnīg būd ud framūd 12000 asb ī tāzīg az ham mōy[111] padisār pad zarr ud morwārīd ud 12000 mard ī juwān[112] kē pad wizīn[113] ī az ērānšahr 12000 zrēh ī haft-gardag[114] ud 12000 šamšēr ī pōlāwadēn[115] ī wirāst

106. S adds in brackets W pnč šh Y YWM W LAYLYA-yh
107. MK, JA, S missing
108. MU ANŠWTA'n
109. MU omits the entire bracket
110. MU AMT
111. S MNW : MU followed by MNW
112. MK ywyn : MU ywb'nc
113. MU OD
114. S glt : MU glt after number 6
115. MU pwl'ptynk

hindūg ud 12000 kamar ī haft čašmag ud abārīg har čē andar 12000 mard ud asp abāyist har čē abrangīgtar payrāyēnīdan. 33) wuzurgmihr ī bōxtagān abar awēšān sālār kard ud rōzgār-ēw wizīdag pad[116] nēk jahišn ud yazdān ayārīh ō hindūgān frēstīd. 34) dēbšalm ī wuzurg šahryār ī hindūgān-šāh ka āwēšān pad ān ēwēnag dīd az wuzurgmihr ī bōxtagān 40 rōz zamān xwāst. 35) ēč kas nē būd az dānāgān ī hindūgān kē čim ī ān nēw-ardaxšīr dānist. 36) wuzurgmihr did-iz[117] ham čand ān sāk ud bāj az dēbšalm stād ud pad nēk jahišn ud wuzurg abrang abāz ō[118] ērānšahr[119] āmad. 37) wizārišn čim ī čatrang ēn kū čē[rī]h pad[120] nērang az ān čiyōn dānāgān-iz guft ēstēd kū pērōz kū[121] pad xrad barēd az ān ī a-zēn[122] [ardīg[123] mādagwarīh ī dānistan][124]. 38) wāzīdan ī čatrang ēn kū nigerišn ud tuxšišn ī pad nigāh dāštan ī abzār ī xwad wēš tuxšišn čiyōn ō burdan šāyistan ī abzār ī ōy did ud pad ummēd ī abzār ī ōy ī did burdan šāyistan rāy dast ī wad nē wāzišn ud hamwār abzār ēk-ēw

116. MU WN
117. S TWB : MU omits
118. MU omits
119. MU štl'
120. MU omits
121. S & MU omits
122. S zyn'
123. S 'tyk
124. MU omits the entire bracket

pad kār ud abārīg pad pahrēz dārišn ud nigerišn bowandag[125]-menišnīhā ud abārīg ōwōn čiyōn andar ēwēnag-nāmag nibišt[126] ēstēd. 39) frazaft pad drōd ud šādīh[127].

125. S bwnyk
126. S & MU fr'c OL
127. S & MU omits the last sentence

English Translation

In the name of the Gods

1) It is said that during the reign of Khusro, of immortal soul,[128] for the sake of testing the wisdom and knowledge of the Iranians[129] and to see his own benefit, Dēbšalm, great sovereign of the Indians, sent one set of chess,[130] 16 pieces

---

128. Anōšag-ruwān "immortal soul" is the honorific epithet given to Khusro I in Middle Persian, Arabic and Persian literature.

129. *ērān-šahrīgān* "Iranians of the Realm / Country," that is the citizens of the empire as opposed to *an-šahrīgān* "foreigners" or "non-citizens."

130. Middle Persian *čatrang* from Sanskrit *caturanga* – "army consisting of four divisions," *hasty-aśva-ratha-padāta* "elephant, horse, chariot, foot soldiers," see P. Thieme, "Chess and Backgammon (Tric-Trac) in Sanskrit Literature," *Indological Studies in Honor of W. Norman Brown*, ed. E. Bender, New Haven Connecticut, 1962, pp. 215, reprint

made from emerald and 16 pieces made from red ruby.

2) Along with that (game of) chess he sent 1200 camel loads of gold and silver and jewels and pearls and goblets[131] (and) 90 elephants and things specially made for them, which were sent along, and Taxtrītos who was notable among the Indians was sent along.

3) In a letter he had written thus: Since you are named king of kings, and over us you are king of kings, then your wise men also must be wiser than ours, either you explain the logic of this (game of) chess or send (us) tribute and tax.

4) The king of kings asked for 3 days, and there was not one among the wise-men in *Ērānšahr* [132] who was able to explain the logic of that chess (game).

5) On the third day, Wuzurgmihr, the son of Boxtag stood upon his feet.

---

in his *Kleine Schriften*, teil 2, Franz Steiner Verlag Gmbh, Wiesbaden, 1971, p. 424.

131. My suggestion in reading *jām* rather than *jāmag* is based on MK and also the *MTQ* and the *ŠN* which is discussed in the introduction.

132. *Ērānšahr* meaning the "Realm" or "Empire of the Iranians" and was the official name of the Sasanian Empire, see G. Gnoli, "Ēr mazdēsn: Zum Begriff Iran und seiner Entstehung im 3. Jahrhundert," in *Transition Periods in Iranian History*, Studia Iranica, Cahier 5, Leuven, 1987, p. 89.

6) He said thus: May you be immortal, I did not explain the logic of this game of chess till today for that reason so that you and anyone who is in *Ērānšahr* know that I am the wisest in *Ērānšahr*.

7) I will easily explain the logic of this (game of) chess and will take tribute and tax from Dēbšalm, and I will create and send something to Dēbšalm which he will not be able to explain, (and) for the second time I will again take tribute and therefore it will become certain that you are worthy of the kingship and our wise-men are wiser than those of Dēbšalm.

8) The king of kings said 3 times thus: Bravo Wuzurgmihr, our Taxtrītos, and he commanded to give Wuzurgmihr 12000 silver coins.[133]

9) On the second day Wuzurgmihr called Taxtrītos before him and said thus: Dēbšalm has designed this chess (game) like a battle in purpose.

10) He made the king like the two overlords at the centre, the rook[134] (on) the left and right flank, the Vazīr[135] like the Commander

---

133. *drahm* from Greek δραχμή. A silver coin weighing 4.25 grams, see Nyberg, 1974, p. 65.

134. *raxw* "rook"

135. *frazēn* "Vazīr" or "Minister"

of the Warriors,[136] the elephant[137] is like the Commander of the Bodyguards,[138] and the horse is like the Commander of the Cavalry,[139] the foot-soldier like the same pawn, that is at front of the battle(field).

11) Then Taxtrītos set the (game of) chess and played with Wuzurgmihr, and Wuzurgmihr won 3 hands from Taxtrītos, and because of this, great joy came to the country.

12) Then Taxtrītos stood upon his feet.

13) He said thus: May you be immortal, God has given you this miraculous power, and glory and strength, and victoriousness. You are the

---

136. *artēštārān-sālār* "Commander of the Warriors," is attested in the Sasanian period from the fifth century CE. Artēštār "warrior" goes back to Avestan *raθaēštā, Les noms racines de l'Avesta*, Wiesbaden, 1974. *Encyclopaedia Iranica*

137. *pīl* "elephant"

138. *puštībānān-sālār* "Commander of the Bodyguards." The office is attested during the reign of king Pērōz as the highest rank in an army sent against the Armenians (Armenian) *p'uštipanan sałar*, *The History of Łazar P'arpec'i*, translated by R.W. Thomson, Scholars Press, Atlanta, 1991, 128-129, pp. 184-185.

139. *aswārān-sālār* "Commander of the Cavalry." For the appearance of the cavalry in the Sasanian period, specifically in the Middle Persian papyri, see D. Weber, "On Middle Persian aswār 'horseman, rider' in Pahlavi Documents of the 7th Century," *Nāme-ye Iran-e Bāstān*, Nos. 11/12, 2006-2007, pp. 37-44.

lord of *Ērān* and *non-Ērān.*[140]

14) Several of the Indian wise-men prepared this set of chess (pieces) with much effort, and toil brought it to this place, (and) no one was able to (give an) explanation.

15) Your Wuzurgmihr due to his innate wisdom rather so easily and simply explained it.

16) He dispatched that much wealth to the treasury of the king of kings.

17) The next day the king of kings called Wuzurgmihr before him.

18) He said to Wuzurgmihr thus: Our Wuzurgmihr, what is that thing which you said to me: I will make and send it to Dēbšalm?

19) Wuzurgmihr said thus: Among the rulers of this millennium Ardaxšīr[141] was more capable

140. *ērān ud anērān xwadāy hēd,* literally "you are the lord of Iranians and non-Iranians." On the concept of *ērān ud an-ērān*, see, G. Gnoli, *The Idea of Iran*, IsMEO, Rome, 1989, p. 129; also Gnoli, *op. cit.,* p. 91. On the title appearing with Šābuhr I, see M.P. Canepa, *The Two Eyes of the Earth. Art and Ritual of Kingship between Rome and Sasanian Iran*, University of California Press, 2009, pp. 54-55. On the concept of *xwadāy* in Middle Persian and the Sasanian period, see M.R. Shayegan, "The Evolution of the Concept of xwadāy "God," *Acta Orientalia Academiae Scientiarum Hungaricae*, 51, no. 1-2 (1998): pp. 31-54.

141. This is in reference to Ardaxšīr I (224-240 CE), the founder of the Sasanian Empire. For his importance and connection to Khusro I, see T. Daryaee, "The Ideal King in the Sasanian World: Ardaxšīr ī Pābagān or Xusrō Anōšag-

and most wise and I will name this (game) backgammon[142] (*Nēw-Ardaxšīr*)[143] in Ardaxšīr's name.

20) I will make the board of the backgammon like the *Spandarmad*[144] earth.

21) and I will make 30 pieces like the 30 night and day, I will make 15 white, like the day, and I will make 15 black, like the night.

22) I will make one single die as the turning of the constellations and the revolution of the firmament.

23) I will make the one on the dice like Ohrmzad, who is one and all goodness was created by him.

24) I will make the two like the spiritual and the material world.

---

ruwān?," *Nāme-ye Iran-e Bāstān*, vol. 5, 2003, pp. 33-46.

142. The earliest mention of backgammon in India occurs in Bhartr,hari's *Vairāgyaśataka* (39) composed around the late sixth or early seventh century CE, see Thieme, *op. cit.*, pp. 423-424. For the history of the game see I. Finkel, "The World Conqueror Emerges: Backgammon in Persia," in *Asian Games: The Art of Contest*, ed. C. MacKenzie and I. Finkel, New York, 2004, pp. 88-95.

143. *Nēw-Ardaxšīr* > (Persian) *nard* or *nardašīr* (also in Arabic), and found in (Babylonian Talmud) *nrdšyr*.

144. *Spandarmad* (Avestan *Spəntā Ārmaiti-*) is one of the *Amahrspandān* "Bounteous Immortals" associated with the earth, hence known as the "goddess of the earth," see Nyberg, 1974, p. 177.

25) I will make the three like good thoughts, good words, and good deeds, and thoughts, words, and deeds.

26) I will make the four like the four elements[145] which the people are made of, and (like) the four corners of the world, northeast and southwest, and southeast, and northwest.

27) I will make the five like the five lights, like the sun, and the moon, and the stars, and the fire and the heavenly brightness which descends from the sky.

28) I will make the six like the creation of the creatures during the six periods of *Gāhānbārs*.[146]

29) I will make the arrangements of the (game of) backgammon on the board like the Lord Ohrmazd, when He created the creatures of the material world.

30) The turning and revolution of the pieces by the die is like people in the material world, their bond[147] connected to the spiritual world,

---

145. *čahār āmēzišn* "four elements" or "humors" which constitute the human body, rendering Persian and Arabic مزاج

146. *Gāhānbār* is the festival connected with one of the six seasonal feasts of the year, Nyberg, 1974, p. 80.

147. *band* "bond" here is the Pahlavi equivalent of the Vedic Sanskrit *bandhu-* which is used as a tie between the human, natural, and divine, see Y.S.-D. Vevaina, "'Enumerating the Dēn': Textual Taxonomies, Cosmological Deixis, and Numerological Speculations in Zoroastrianism," *History of*

through the 7 and 12 (planets and constellation) they all have their being and move on, and when it is as if they hit one against another and collect, it is like people in the material world, one hits another (person).

31) And when by the turning of this die all are collected, it is in the likeness of the people who all passed out from the material world (died), and when they set them up again, it is in the likeness of the people who during the (time of) resurrection, all will come to life again.

32) When the king of kings heard that speech, he became joyful and commanded 12,000 Arabian horses of the same hair (color), bridled with gold and pearls and 12,000 young men[148] who are distinguished in *Ērānšahr*, 12,000 coat of mail armor of seven-fold[149] and 12,000

Religions 50/2, 2010, pp. 127-128.

148. *mard ī juwān* "young man," which I believe refers to the specific institution known in Iran as جوانمردی, hence the medieval idea of عیّاری. These men were used in the Sasanian military and then joined the Muslim armies, see M. Zakeri, *Sāsānid Soldiers in Early Muslim Society. The Origins of 'Ayyārān and Futuwwa*, Harrassowitz Verlag, Wiesbaden, 1995. For their function in the medieval Iranian society see, M. Afšārī, *Čahārdah resaleh dar bāb-e futuvat va asnāf*, Tehran, 1381; and also his, *Futuvatnāmeh-hā va rasā'il khāksārīyeh*, Tehran, 1382.

149. *haft-gardag*, armor in Iran was made by banding brass scales or linen which was tied together. Here the sense is

swords prepared of Indian steel, (and) 12,000 seven-jeweled belts[150] and whatever is needed for 12,000 men (and) horses, everything adorned in the most splendid manner.

33) Wuzurgmihr, the son of Boxtag was made commander over them, and at the chosen date, with good fortune and with the aid of the Gods, sent to the Indians.

34) Dēbšalm the great, the sovereign of the king of the Indians, when he saw them in that manner, he asked Wuzurgmihr, the son of Boxtag for 40 days time.

---

that a thick armor which has probably seven layers or folds of protection is mentioned, Nyberg, 1974, p. 113.

150. *kamar-e haft češmeh* appears in Persian literature, meaning that there were belts with seven studs or jewels for those of rank and status. In *Haft Peykar* Nezāmī, Bahrām Gūr is made king in such a manner:

They placed the crown on his head تاج بر فرق سر نهادندش
They gave to him the belt of seven gems کمر هفت چشمه دادندش

This belt is associated with the Kayanid kings in Persian literature where it has seven jewels, each having a particular color and corresponding to the seven planets, see C.E. Wilson, *The Haft Paikar (The Seven Beauties), Containing the Life and Adventures of King Bahrām Gūr, and the Seven Stories Told him by his Seven Queens*, Stephen Austin and Sons, London, 1924, (online). See, A. Taffazoli, "Kamar-e Haft Češmeh," *Iranšenāsī*, vol. 27, 1374, pp. 495-496.

35) There was no one among the wise-men of the Indians who knew the logic of that (game of) backgammon.

36) Wuzurgmihr again collected as much tribute and tax from Dēbšalm and through good fortune and great splendor returned to *Ērānšahr*.

37) The explanation (of) the logic of chess is this: Victory through skill, in the manner which the wise have said: The victor who wins through wisdom, from having the essential knowledge of weaponless war.

38) The explanation of chess is this that, observation and striving through protecting one's own piece, greater striving to be able to capture the other person's pieces, not playing a bad hand because of hope of being able to capture the other person's pieces, always keeping one piece on the attack and the others on the defense, observing with complete mindfulness, and other as has been written in the *Book of Manners*.[151]

39) Completed with salutation and joy.

---

151. In Arabic this genre came to be known as كتاب الآيين concerned with manuals on various arts and sciences such as archery, polo, dining, translated from Middle Persian into Arabic, etc., see A. Tafazzolī, *Tārīkh-e adabiyāt Irān piš az Islam*, Tehran, 1376, p. 266; see also K. Mazdapour's introduction to M. Afšārī, *Tāzeh be tāzeh, now be now*, Sokhan Publishers, Tehran, 1384, pp. 12-13.

JA MANUSCRIPT

[illegible]

۱ [illegible]
[illegible]
[illegible]
[illegible]
۲ [illegible]
[illegible]
[illegible]
[illegible]
[illegible]

۳ [illegible]
[illegible]
[illegible]
[illegible]

۴ [illegible]
[illegible]
[illegible]

---

1 In TD the text 'Darakht-i asûrik' is not copied; the copyist makes a note of the omission stating in Persian قصر یک مانده است. 2 TD, JJ [illegible]. TD [illegible]. 4 MK, JJ [illegible]. 5 MK,JJ om. 6 MK, JJ [illegible]. 7 MK, JJ [illegible]. 8 MK, JJ [illegible]. 9 TD [illegible]. 10 JJ [illegible]. 11 TD [illegible]. 12 JJ [illegible]. 13 TD [illegible]. 14 JJ [illegible].

116 [illegible]
5 [illegible]
6 [illegible]
[illegible]
[illegible]
7 [illegible]
[illegible]
[illegible]
[illegible]
[illegible]
[illegible]
8 [illegible]
[illegible]
[illegible]

9 [illegible]
[illegible]
10 [illegible]
[illegible]
[illegible]

---

15 MK, JJ om. 16 MK, JJ [illegible]. 17 JJ [illegible]. 18 MK, TD [illegible]. 19 MK [illegible]. 20 MK, JJ [illegible]. 21 JJ omits [illegible]. 22 MK, JJ prefix [illegible]. 23 JJ omits. 24 MK, JJ [illegible]. 25 MK [illegible]. 26 JJ omits [illegible]. 27 TD [illegible]. 28 TD [illegible]. 29 TD [illegible]. 30 JJ prefixes [illegible], which is written and struck off in MK. 31 MK [illegible]. 32 TD [illegible]. 33–34 TD omits.

۱۱۷ [illegible]
[illegible]
۱۱ [illegible]
[illegible]
[illegible]
[illegible]

۱۲ [illegible]
۱۳ [illegible]
[illegible]
۱۴ [illegible]
[illegible]
[illegible]
۱۵ [illegible]
[illegible]
۱۶ [illegible]
[illegible]

۱۷ [illegible]
۱۸ [illegible]
[illegible]
[illegible]

---

35 MK, JJ om. 36 TD [illegible]. 37 TD omits. 38 TD [illegible]. 39 MK [illegible]. 40 MK [illegible]. 41 JJ [illegible]. 42 MK, JJ [illegible]. 43 MK, JJ [illegible]. 44 MK, TD [illegible]; JJ [illegible]. 45 TD [illegible]. 46 JJ [illegible]; TD [illegible]. 47 MK, JJ [illegible].

۱۸ [illegible]

۱۹ [illegible]

[illegible]

۲۰ [illegible]

۲۱ [illegible]

[illegible]

[illegible]

۲۲ [illegible]

۲۳ [illegible]

[illegible]

۲۴ [illegible]

۲۵ [illegible]

۲۶ [illegible]

[illegible]

[illegible]

۲۷ [illegible]

[illegible]

۲۸ [illegible]

۲۹ [illegible]

---

48 MK, JJ [illegible]. 49-50 TD omits. 51 JJ [illegible]. 52 MK [illegible]. 53 MK, JJ [illegible] with [illegible] written above [illegible]. 54 MK, JJ [illegible]. 55 Written and struck off in TD. 56 JJ omits. 57 MK torn; JJ, TD [illegible]. 58 TD [illegible]. 59 MK, JJ om. 60 TD [illegible]. 61 MK omits. 62 MK, JJ om. [illegible]. 63 MK, JJ [illegible]. 64 MK, JJ [illegible]. 65 JJ [illegible].

[illegible]
[illegible]
۳۰ [illegible]
[illegible]
[illegible]
[illegible]
[illegible]
۳۱ [illegible]
[illegible]
[illegible]
[illegible]
۳۲ [illegible]
[illegible]
[illegible]
[illegible]
[illegible]
[illegible]
[illegible]
۳۳ [illegible]
[illegible]

---

66 TD [illegible]. 67 MK [illegible]. 68 TD [illegible]. 69 JJ [illegible]. 70 MK [illegible]. 71 MK [illegible]. 72 JJ omits. 73 JJ [illegible]. 74 TD [illegible]. 75 JJ [illegible]; TD [illegible]. 76 MK [illegible]; TD [illegible]. 77 JJ [illegible]. 78 TD [illegible]. 79 MK, JJ om. 80 TD [illegible]. 81 MK [illegible]. 82 TD [illegible]. 83 MK [illegible]; JJ [illegible]. 84 TD [illegible]. 85 MK, JJ [illegible]. 86 TD [illegible].

[illegible] ١٢٠

[illegible] ٣٤

[illegible]

[illegible] ٣٥

[illegible] ٣٦

[illegible]

[illegible]

[illegible] ٣٧

[illegible]

[illegible]

[illegible] ٣٨

[illegible]

[illegible]

[illegible]

[illegible]

[illegible]

[illegible]

[illegible]

[illegible]

87–88 MK, JJ om. 89 JJ [illegible]. 90 JJ [illegible]. 91 TD [illegible]. 92 TD [illegible]. 93 TD [illegible]. 94 MK, JJ om. 95 JJ omits [illegible]. 96 TD [illegible]. 97 TD omits. 98 TD [illegible]. 99 TD [illegible]. 100 TD [illegible]. 1 TD [illegible]. 2–3 TD [illegible]. 4 JJ [illegible]. 5 TD adds [illegible].

MU2 MANUSCRIPT

١٣٨

۱۲۹

١٤٠

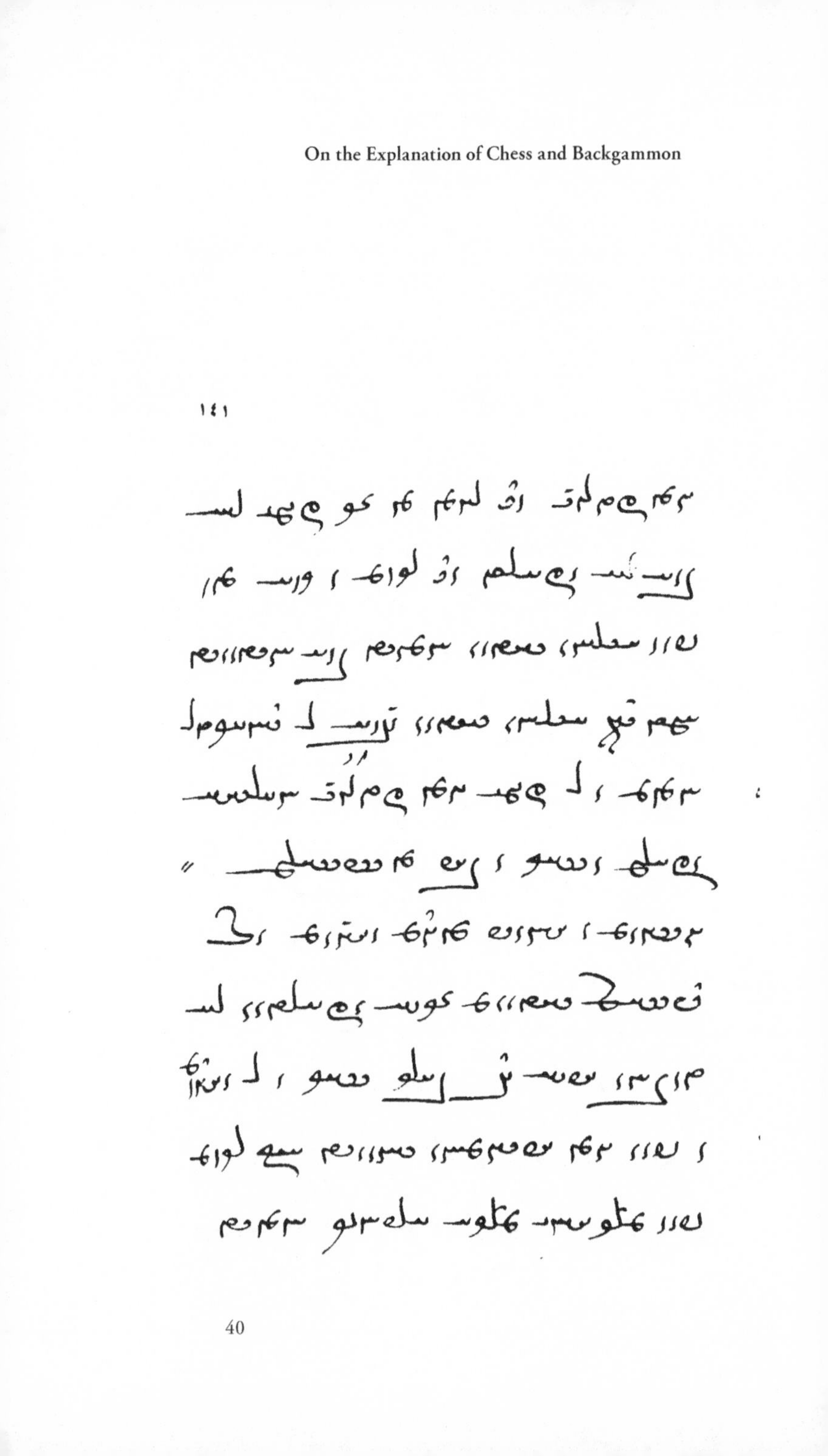

١٤١

١٤٢

١٤٣

١٤٤

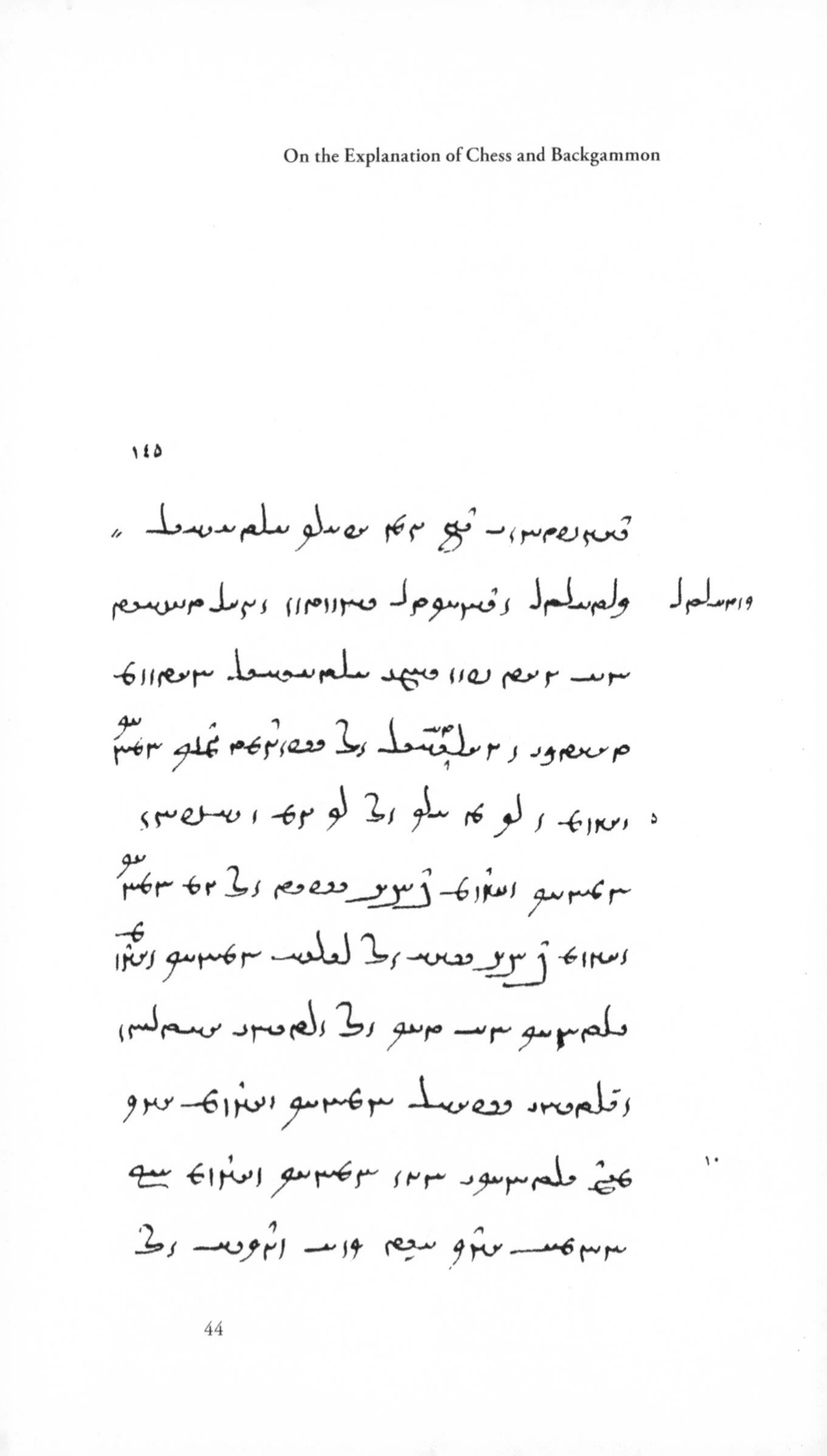

١٤٥

١٤٦

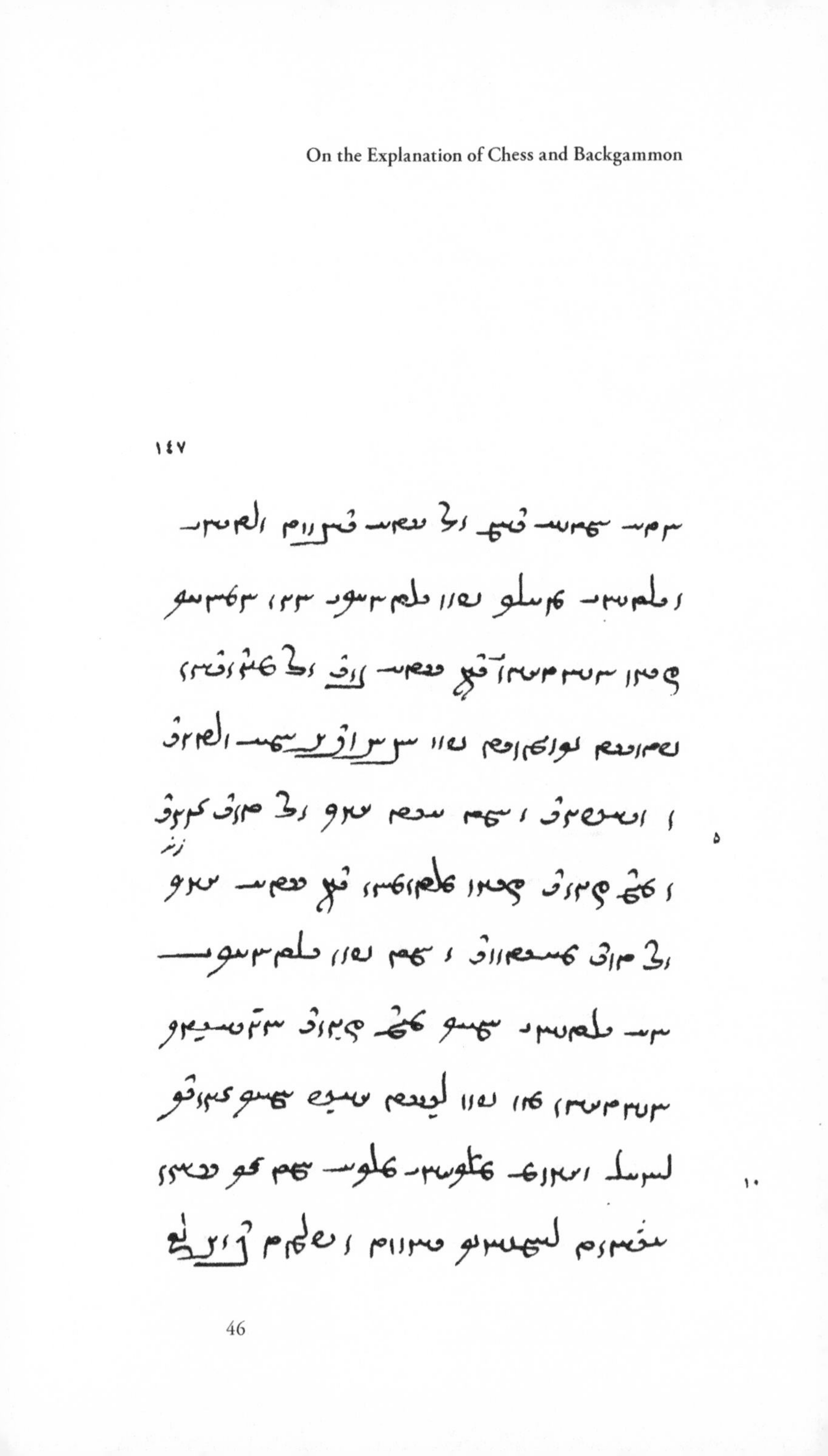

١٤٧

١٤٨

١٤٩

[illegible]

۱۵۰

S MANUSCRIPT

[illegible]

૧ [illegible]
[illegible]
[illegible]
[illegible]
[illegible]
[illegible]
[illegible]
[illegible]
[illegible]
[illegible]
[illegible]
૨ [illegible]
[illegible]
૩ [illegible]
[illegible]
[illegible]
[illegible]

---

૧. ૧) બેહુ નકલમાં [illegible] મલેછે.
૧. ૨) દ. કે. વાલી નકલમાં [illegible] મલેછે.
૧. ૩) દ. કે. વાલી નકલમાં [illegible] મલેછે.
૧. ૪) દ. કે. વાલી નકલમાં [illegible] મલેછે.
૧. ૫) દ. કે. વાલી નકલમાં [illegible] મલેછે.
૧. ૬) આએ નીચાંન ફકરો જુદો પાડવા સારૂ હમારી તરફથી મેલીછે.

(૨)

[illegible]
[illegible]
[illegible]
[illegible]
[illegible]
[illegible]
[illegible] ૪
[illegible]
[illegible] ૫
[illegible]
[illegible]
[illegible]
[illegible]
[illegible]
[illegible]
[illegible]
[illegible] ૬
[illegible]
[illegible]

૩. ૧) બેહુ નકલમાં [illegible] મલેછે.
૩. ૨) દ. હૃ. તથા દ. કે. વાલી બંને નકલમાં [illegible] હતું તેહને હમોએ સુધારીછે.
૪. ૧) બંને નકલમાં [illegible] મલેછે. ૨) બેહુ નકલમાં [illegible] છે.
૫. ૧) દ. કૈખુસરો વાલી નકલમાં [illegible] મલેછે.
૫. ૨) બેહુ નકલમાં [illegible] છે.
૫. ૩) દ. હૃ. તથા દ. કે. વાલી બેહુ નકલમાં [illegible] મલેછે.
૫. ૪) બંને નકલમાં [illegible] છે. ૫) બેહુ કેતાબમાં [illegible] નું લખાંણ મલેછે.
૬. ૧) એક સરખી રીતે બેહુ નકલમાં [illegible] મલેછે.

(૩)

[illegible] ૭
[illegible]
[illegible]
[illegible]
[illegible]
[illegible] ૮
[illegible]
[illegible]
[illegible] ૯
[illegible]
[illegible]
[illegible]
[illegible]
[illegible]
[illegible]
[illegible] ૧૦
[illegible]
[illegible] ૧૧
[illegible] ૧૨
[illegible] ૧૩

---

૭. ૧) બેહુ નકલમાં [illegible] છે.　　૨) બેહુમાં [illegible] મલેછે.
૮. ૧) દ. રૂ. તથા દ. કે. વાલી નકલમાં [illegible] છે.
૮. ૨) દ. કે. વાલી નકલમાં [illegible] છે.
૯. ૧) બેહુ નકલમાં [illegible] મલેછે.　　૨) બંને નકલમાં [illegible] મલેછે.
૯. ૩) બેહુ કેતાબમાં [illegible] છે.　　૪) બંને નકલમાં [illegible] મલેછે.
૯. ૫) આ ફકરો જુદો પાડેલો બેહુ નકલમાં મલતો નથી.
૧૦. ૧) આએ બોલ બેહુ નકલમાં નથી.
૧૦. ૨) દ. કે. વાલી નકલમાં [illegible] મલેછે.

(۴)

[illegible]
[illegible] ૧૪
[illegible]
[illegible] ૧૫
[illegible]
[illegible] ૧૬
[illegible]
[illegible] ૧૭
[illegible]
[illegible]
[illegible]
[illegible] ૧૮
[illegible]
[illegible]
[illegible]
[illegible] ૧૯
[illegible]
[illegible]

---

૧૩. ૧) આએ [illegible] બેાઝને બદલે બેહુ નકલમાં [illegible] મલેછે.
૧૪. ૧) દ. કે. વાલી નકલમાં [illegible] છે.
૧૪. ૨) આએ એબારત અસલ લખાંણમાંથી નીકલી ગએલી સહમજીને હમોએ તે વધારેલીછે.
૧૫. ૧) આએ ફકરેા પુરેા થવાની નીશાંની બંને નકલોમાં મલતી નથી.
૧૬. ૧) બંને નકલમાં [illegible] મલેછે.
૧૭. ૧) બેહુ નકલમાં [illegible] મલેછે.
૧૭. ૨) દ. કે. વાલી નકલમાં [illegible] છે. ૩) બંને નકલમાં [illegible] મલેછે.
૧૭. ૪) આએ વધાએઆમાંની એબારત નકલ કરનારની તરફથી નીકલી ગએલી હોવી જોઇએ.
૧૯. ૧) બેહુ નકલમાં [illegible] મલેછે, અને ફકરેા જુદેા પાડેલેા નથી.

Glossary

A

abāg	[LWTE] "with" : 2; 11
abar	[QDM] "up, on": 5; 12; 23; 29; 31; 33
abārīg	['p'ryk'] "other": 32; 38
abāxtar	['p'htl] "northwest": 26
abāyed	['p'yt'] "must, fitting, necessary": 3
abāyist	['p'yst'] "necessary, needed": 32
abāz	[LAWHL] "again": 31; 36
abēgumān	['pygwm'n'] "certain": 7
abrang	['plng] "glory, splendor" 36
abrangīgtar	['plnkyktl] "most splendid": 32
abzār	['pz'l] "instrument,

	piece": 38
agar	[HT] "if": 3
amā	[LNE] "we": 3; 7
āmadan / āy-	[YATWN-tn'] "come": 27; 36
amāwandīh	['m'wndyh] "strength": 13
āmēzišn	['mycšn'] "elements": 26
ān	[ZK] "that: 16; 37
and	['nd] "so much, many": 16
andar	[BYN] "among, in": 1; 2; 6; 30; 32; 38
anērān	['n'yl'n'] "Non-Iran": 13
anōšag	['nwšk']"immortal":6;13
anōšag-ruwān	['nwšk-lwb'n] "immortal soul": 1
ardaxšīr	['lthšyl] "Ardaxšīr": 19
ardīg	['ltyk'] "war, battle": 37
artēštārān-sālār	['ltyšt'l'n-srd'l] "commander of the warriors": 10
arzānīg	['lc'nyk'] "worthy": 7
asēm	['sym] "silver": 2
asmān	['sm'n'] "sky" 27
āsnxrad	['snhlt'] "innate wisdom": 15
asp	[SWSYA] "horse": 10; 32
ast	[AYT] "is, exists": 18; 23; 30
aswārān-sālār	['swb'l'n'-srd'l] "commander of the cavalry":10

ašmā	[LKWM] "you": 3, 6, 7, 14, 15
ašnūd	['šnwt] "heard": 32
ātaxš	['thš] "fire": 27
awēšān	[OLEš'n] "they, those": 33; 34
āwurd	[YHYTYWN-t'] "brought": 14
axtarān	['hltl'n] "stele, constellation": 22
ayārīh	[hdyb'lyh] "aid, help": 33
az	[MN] "from": 1; 7; 11; 19; 26; 27; 31; 32; 34; 35; 36; 37
a-zēn	['zyn] "weaponless": 37

B

band	[bnd] "bond": 30
bāj	[b'c] "tribute": 3; 7; 36
bār	[b'l] "time, occasion": 8
bār	[b'l] "load": 2
bārag	[b'lk'] "double": 7
barēd	[YBLWN-šn] "win, victory": 37
be	[BRA] participle with verbs: 6; 15; 31
bowandag-mēnišnīhā	[bwndk'-mynyšnyh'] "complete mindfulness": 38

būd, b(aw)-	[YHWWN-t', bwt'] "be": 2; 3; 6; 13;14; 19; 31; 32; 35
burdan, bar-	[YBLWN-tn'] "take, carry": 11; 37; 38

C

čahār	[4] "four, 4": 26
čand	[cnd] "few, several, much, many": 14; 36
čašmag	[cšmk'] "jeweled, studded": 32
čatrang	[ctlng] "chess": 1; 2; 3; 4; 5; 7; 11; 14; 37; 38
čē	[ME] "because, since": 18; 32
čehel	[40] "forty, 40": 34
čērīh	[cylyh] "victory": 37
čīdan, cīn	[cytn'] "gather, pile up, pass": 30; 31
čim	[cym] "reason, logic": 3; 4; 5; 7; 9; 35; 37
čiš	[MNDOM] "thing, affair": 2; 18; 37
čiyōn	[cygwn'] "in this way, manner": 2; 3; 24;25; 26; 27; 29; 30; 37; 38

D

dādan, dah-	[YHBWN-tn'; dh-] "give" 8; 23; 28; 29
dahibedān	[dhywpt'n] "rulers": 19
dām	[d'm] "creation": 28
dānāgān	[d'n'k'n'] "wise men, sages" 3; 4; 5-6; 7; 14; 35; 37
dānāgdar	[d'n'ktl] "piu sapient" "wiser" : 3; 7; 19
dānāgih	[d'n'kyh] "wisdom": 1
dānistan, dān-	[YDOYTWN-stn; d'n-] "knowledge, know": 6; 35; 37
dārišn	[YHSNNšn] "keep, hold, preserve": 38
dast	[YDE] "hand" : 38
dāštan, dār-	[YHSNN-tn'; d'stn', d'l-] "have, hold": 38
dwāzdah	[12] "twelve, 12" : 30
dwāzdah hazār	[12,000] "twelve thousand": 8; 32
dēbšalm	[dypšlm] "Dēbšalm": 1; 7; 8; 9; 17-18; 34; 36
did	[TWB] "again": 30; 36; 38
dō	[2, TLYN'] "2, two": 7; 10; 24
drahm	[ZWZN] "drahm": 8

drōd	[ŠRM, dlwt'] "salutation" ending formula
dudīgar	[dtykl] "second": 9; 17

E

ēč	['yc] "no one, not one": 4; 14; 35
ēdōn	['ytwn'] "in this manner, in this way": 1; 15; 29; 37
ēk	['ywk] "one" : 23; 30; 38
ēn	[ZNE; 'ywk] "this" passim.
ēnyā	['yny'] "otherwise, or": 3
ērān	['yl'n] "Iranians": 1; 13
ērānšahr	['yl'nštr'] "Ērānšahr, Realm of the Iranians, Sasanian Empire" : 4; 6; 32; 36
ērānšahrīgān	['yl'nštr'yk'n'] "Iranians, inhabitants of Ērānšahr": 1
estādan, est-	[YKOYMWN-tn'] "be": 5; 12; 30; 37
ē(w)	[HD, I] "1, one": 1; 7; 14; 19; 22; 23; 30; 31; 38
ēwēnag	['dwynk] "custom, manner": 34; 38
ēw-tāg	['ywt'k'] "one single (die)": 22

F

framūdan, framāy-	[plmwtn', plm'd-] "command, order": 8; 32
frawardag	[plwltk'] "letter": 3
frazāft	[prc'pt] "finite" Finis
frazēn	[plcyn'] "Vazīr, minister": 10
frēstādan, frēst-	[ŠDRWN-(y)tn'] "send": 1; 2; 3; 7; 18

G

gāh	[g's] "period, time": 28
gāhānbār	[g's'nb'l] "the six divisions of the year": 28
ganj	[gnc] "treasure" : 16
gardānāg	[glt'n'k'] "die": 22; 23; 30; 31
gardišn	[gltyšn'] "turning": 22; 30; 31
gētīg	[gytyk] "material (world)": 24; 26; 29; 30; 31
gōwišn	[gwbšn] "words" : 25
griftan, gīr-	[OHDWN-tn'; gyl-] "take": 7
guftan, go(w)-	[YMRRWN-, YMLLWN-tn'] "say, speak": 1; 6; 8; 12-13; 17-18;

	19; 37
gōhr	[gwhl] "jewel": 2
gyāg	[gyw'k'] "place": 14

H

haft	[7] = "seven, 7": 30; 32
haft-čašmag	[7-cšmk] "seven-jeweled ": 32
haft-gardag	[7-grtk] "(pounded) seven-fold": 32
ham	[hm] "same, similar": 10; 36
hamāg	[hm'k'] "all": 3; 11; 30
ham-mōy	[hm-mwd] "same hair": 32
hamwār	[hmw'l] "always": 38
hangōšīdag	[hngwšytk'] "likeness, way, manner": 31
harg	[hlg] "effort, work": 14
har(w)	[KRA] "all, each, every ": 6; 23; 32
hazār ud dō-sad	[1200] "twelve hundred, 1200": 2
hazārag	[hc'lk'] "millennium": 19
hindūg	[hndwk'] "Indian": 32
hindūgān	[hndwk'n] "Indians": 1, 2, 14; 33; 34, 35
homānāg	[h(w)m'n'k'] "like, likeness": 9; 10; 20; 22; 23;

	24; 25; 26; 27; 28; 29; 30
humat	[hwnt'] "good thought": 25
husraw anōšag-ruwān	[hwslwb 'nwšk-lwb'n] "Khusro of immortal soul": 1
huwaršt	[hwwlšt'] "good deed": 25
hūxt	[hwht'] "good word" 25

I

ī	[Y, ZY-] rel. pron. "who, which": passim
im	[LZNE] "this": 6
-iz	[-(y)c] adv. enclitic "also, even": 1; 7; 31

J

jām	[y'm] "vessel, goblet": 2
juwān	[ywb'n'] "youth, young": 32
juxt	[ywht'] "pair": 14; 19

K

ka	[AMT] "when, if, since": 29; 30; 31; 32; 34
kamar	[kml] "belt": 32

kār	[k'l] "work": 38
kardan, kun-	[OBYDWN-tn', kwn-] "do, act, make":1; 9; 10; 15-16; 17-18; 21; 22; 23; 24; 25; 26; 27; 28; 29; 32; 33.
kardārtar	[klt'ltl] "capable": 19
kārezār	[k'lyc'l] "battle, war": 9
kas	[AYŠ] "person, somebody": 4; 14; 35
kē	[MNW] "who, which": 4; 6; 26; 31; 32; 35
kišwar	[kyšwl] "country, realm, clime": 11
kū	[AYK] "where, that, then"1; 3; 6; 7; 8;13; 18; 19; 23; 37; 38
kunišn	[kwnšn'] "action, deed, make": 25

M

mādagīg	[m'tkyk'] "special, essential": 2
mādagwarīhā	[m'tkwlyh'] "especial, essential": 37
madan	[mtn'] "come": 11
mādayārān	[m'tgd'l'n] "centre, core, main": 10

māh	[BYRH] "moon": 27
man	[L] = "I": 6; 7
mard	[GBRA] "man": 6; 32
mardōm	[ANŠWTA, mltwm] "people, human": 26; 30; 31
mardōmān	[mltwm'n] "people": 31
menišn	[mynšn'] "though": 25
mēnōg	[mynwk] "spiritual (world)": 24
mēnōgān	[mynwk'n] "spiritual": 30
morwārīd	[mwlw'lyt'] "pearl": 1; 32
muhrag	[mwhlk'] (backgammon playing) "piece": 21; 30

N

nām	[ŠM; n'm] "name" 3; 19
nāmag	[MGLTA, n'mk'] "book" : 38
nawad	[90] "ninety, 90": 2
nē	[LA] "no": 4; 35
nēk-jahišn	[nywk-yhyšn] "good fortune": 33; 36
nēkīh	[nywkyh] "goodness": 23
nēmrōz	[nym-lwc] "southeast": 26
nērang	[nylng] "skill, trickery": 37
nēw-ardaxšīr	[nyw'lthšyl] "backgammon": 19; 29; 35

nibištan, nibēs-	[YKTYBWN-stn'] “to write”: 3
nigāh	[nk’s] “protection, hold”: 38
nigerišn	[nkylšn] “observe”: 38
nihādag	[nyd’tk']=“arrangement”:29
nihādan, nih	[HNHTWN-tn'] “set”: 11; 14; 19; 31

O

ō	[OL] “to, at”: 5; 7; 8; 9; 10; 12-13; 14; 16; 17; 18; 20; 21; 22; 23; 29; 30; 33; 38
ohrmazd	[’whrmzd] “Ohrmazd”: 23; 29
ōwon	[’wgwn] “so, as”: 3; 23; 25; 26; 27; 30; 38

P

pad	[PWN] “to, at, in, on”: 2; 11; 14; 19; 28; 30; 31; 32; 33; 36; 37; 38
padisār	[ptys’l] “bridle, halter”: 32
pahrēz	[p’hlyc] “protect”: 38
panj	[5] “five, 5”: 4; 27
pānzdah	[15] “fifteen, 15”: 21
pas	[AHL] “then”: 11; 12

pāy	[LGLE; p'dy] "foot": 5; 12
payādag	[pd'tk] "pawn": 10
payrāyēnīdan	[pyl'dynytn'] "splendid": 32
paywastan, paywand-	[ptwstn', pywnd-] "to connect, attach": 30
pērōz	[pylwc'] "victory": 37
pērōzgarīh	[pylwcglyh] "victory": 13
pēš	[LOYN'; pyš] "before, front": 9; 10; 17
pīl	[pyl] "elephant": 2
pōlāwadēn	[pwl'ptyn'] "steel": 32
puštībānān	[pwštykp'n'n] "bodyguards": 10
puštībānān-sālār	[pwštykp'n-srd'l] "commander of the bodyguards": 10

R

rāmišn	[l'mšn'] "joy": 11
ramišnīg	[l'mšnyk'] "joyful": 32
ranj	[lnc] "effort, toil": 14
raxw	[lhw'] "rook": 10
rāy	[l'd] "for, for the sake of" postposition: 1; 38
razm	[lcm] "battle": 10
rist-āxēz	[lyst'hyc] "resurrection": 31
rōšnih	[lwšnyh] "light": 27

rōz [YWM; lwc] "day": 4; 5-6; 9; 17; 21; 34
rōzgār [lwck'l] "day, (appointed) date,": 33

S

sabukīhā [spwkyh'] "easily": 15
sāk [s'k'] "tribute": 3; 7; 36
sālār [srd'l] "commander": 10; 33
sarxwadāy [slhwt'y] "overlord": 10
saxwan [MRYA, shwn'] "speech": 32
sē [3] = "three, 3" 4; 8; 11; 25
sidīgar [stykl] "third": 5
sih [30] "thirty, 30": 21
sōg [swk'] "corner, side": 26
spandarmad [spndrmt'] "Spandarmad" "Holy Thought": 20
spēd [spyt'] "white": 21
spihr [spy(y)hl] "firmament": 22
stadan, stān- [YNSBWN-tn'] "take": 7; 36
stārag [st'lk] "star": 27
sūd [swt'] "benefit": 1
suxr [swhl]] "red": 21
syā [syd'] "black": 21
šab [LYLYA; šp] "night": 21
šabān [šp'n] "nights": 21
šādīh [š'tyh] "joy" ending for-

	mula
šāh	[MLKA, šh] "king": 1: 3; 4; 8; 16; 17; 32; 34
šāhān	[MLKAn] "kings": 3; 4; 7; 8; 16; 17; 32
šāhīh	[MLKAyh] "kingship, king": 3
šahrīgān	[štr'yk'n] "residents, citizens": 1
šahryār	[štr'd'l] "sovereign"1; 34
šamšēr	[šmšyl] "sword": 32
šāzdah	[16] "sixteen, 16": 1
šaš	[6] "six, 6": 28
šāyištan, šāy-	[š'dystn'] "worthy": 4; 38

T

tā	[OD] "until, so that": 6; 14
tāg	[t'k'] "piece": 1
taxtag	[t'htk] "board": 19; 29
taxtrītōs	[thtlytws] "Taxtrītos": 2; 9; 11; 12
tāzīg	[t'cyk'] "Arab": 32
tuwān	[twb'n'] "able, power": 7; 14
tuxšīšn	[twhššn'] "to strive, striving": 38

U

ud	[W] "and" passim.
u-š	[AP-Š] enclitic pronoun
ummēd	['wmyt'] "hope, wish": 38
uštar	[GMRA, 'wštl] "camel": 2
uzmūdan, uzmāy-	['wzmwtn'] "test": 1
uzumburd	['wzmbwlt'] "emerald": 1

W

wad	[SLYA, wt'] "bad": 38
wardēnīdan, wardēn-	[wltyn-ytn', wltyn-] "to turn, revolve": 30
wardišn	[wltšn] "turning": 22; 30
warz	[wlc] "miraculous": 13
warzag	[wlck'] "heavenly brightness": 27
was	[KBD] "many": 14
wāzīdan, wāz-	[w'cytn', w'c-] "to play": 11; 38
wēš	[wyš] "more": 38
widerān	[wtyl'n'] "dying, passing away": 31
wihēzēnd	[wyhycnd] "move forward, progress": 30
wirāstan, wirāy-	[wyl'stn', wyl'd-] "arrange, prepare": 32
wisē	[wsydy] "dispatch": 16

wizārdan, wizār-	[wc'l-tn', wc'l-] "explain": 4; 6; 7; 14
wizārišn	[wc'lšn'] "explanation": 37
wizīdag	[wcytk] "choose": 33
wizīdan, wizīn-,	[wcytn', wycn-] "choose, select": 2; 32
wuzurg	[LBA; wc(w)lg] "great": 1; 11; 33; 34; 36
wuzurgmihr ī boxtagān	[wcwlgmtr' Y bwhtk'n] "Wuzurgmihr, son of Boxtag": 5; 8; 11; 15; 17-18; 19; 33; 34; 36

X

xrad	[hlt'] "wisdom": 1
xwad	[BNPŠE] "self": 38
xwadāy	[hwt'y] "Lord": 29
xwadāyīh	[hwt'yyh] "reign, rulership": 1
xwarāsān	[hwl's'n'] "east, northeast": 26
xwārīhā	[hw'lyh'] "easy, simple": 7; 15
xwarrah	[GDH] "glory, splendor": 11
xwaršēd	[hwlšyt] "sun": 27
xwarwarān	[hwlwl'n] "west, northwest": 26

xwāstag	[NKSYA] "welath": 16
xwāstan, xwah-	[BOYHWN-tn'; hw'stn'] "seek, wanted": 9; 17; 34
xwēš	[NPŠE] "own, self": 15; 38

Y

yākand	[y'knd, -nt'] "ruby": 1
yazad	[yzdt'] "god, divinity": 13

Z

zadan, zan-	[MHYTWN-tn', ztn', zn-] "hit, strike, smite": 30
zamān	[ODNA; zm'n'] "time": 4; 34
zamīg	[zmyk'] "earth": 20
zarr	[ZHBA] "gold": 2; 32
zīwā	[zy(w)'] "bravo": 8
zīyandag	[zy(w)ndk'] "alive, living": 31
zrēh	[zlyh] "armor": 32

Bibliography

Afšārī, M. *Čahārdah resaleh dar bāb-e futuvat va asnāf,* Tehran, 1381.

Afšārī, M. *Futuvatnāmeh-hā va rasā'īl khāksārīyeh*, Tehran, 1382.

Amuzegar, J. "Paymān," *The Spirit of Wisdom [Mēnōg ī Xrad]. Essays in Memory of Ahmad Tafazzoli*, eds. T. Daryaee & M. Omidsalar, Mazda Publishers, Costa Mesa, 2004.

Azarnouche, S. *Husraw ī Kawādān ud Rēdag-ē/ Khosrow fils de Kawād et un Page, texte pehlevi édité et traduit par* Samra Azarnouche, Studia Iranica, Cahier 49, Paris, 2013.

Azarpay, G. *Sogdian Painting, The Pictoral Epic in Oriental Art*, University of California Press, Berkeley, Los Angeles and London, 1981.

Bahār, M.T. "Gozāresh-e šatrang va nahādan-e vanirdšēr," *Tarjumeh-ye čand matn-e pahlavī,*" Tehran, 1347, pp. 10-17.

Bailey, H.W. *Zoroastrian Problems in the Ninth-*

Century Books, Oxford, Clarendon Press, 1943.

Barakat, R.A. *Tāwula: A Study in Arabic Folklore*, Suomalainen Tiedeakatemia, Academia Scientiarum Fennica, Helsinki, 1974.

Boyce, M. "Middle Persian Literature," *Handbuch der Orientalistik, Iranistik*, Literatur, Lieferung 1, Leiden / Köln, E.J. Brill, 1968.

Brunner, C.J. "The Middle Persian Explanation of Chess and Invention of Backgammon," *The Journal of the Ancient Near Eastern Society of Columbia University*, Vol. 10, 1978, pp. 43-51.

Brunner, "Astrology and Astronomy II. Astronomy and Astrology in the Sasanian Period," *Encyclopaedia Iranica*, ed. E. Yarshater, Vol. II, Routledge & Kegan Paul, London and New York, 1987, p. 862-868.

Bussagli, M. *Painting of Central Asia*, The World Publishing Company, Ohio, 1963.

Caenpa, M.P. *The Two Eyes of the Earth. Art and Ritual of Kingship between Rome and Sasanian Iran*, University of California Press, 2009.

Cantera, A. Review of A. Panaino's La Novella degli Scacchi e della Tavola Reale, *Orientalistiche Literaturzeitung*, vol. 95, no. 3, 2000, pp. 304-311.

Cereti, C.G. *La letteratura Pahlavi, Introduzione ai testi con riferimenti alla storoia degli studi e alla tradizione manoscritta*, Mimesis, Milano, 2001.

Čahār maghāle, ed. M. Ghazwini and M. Mo'īn, Armaghān Publishers, Tehran, 1331.

Choksy, J.K. "Gesture in Ancient Iran and Central Asia II: Proskynesis and the Bent Forefinger," *Bulletin of the Asia Institute*, Vol. 4, 1990[1992], pp. 201-207.

Christensen, A. "La légende du sage Buzurjmihr," *Acta Orientalia*, Vol. 8, 1929, pp. 81-128.

Chukanova, O.M. *Kniga deianii Ardashira syna Papaka*, Pamiatniki Pis'mennosti Vostoka, Moscow, 1987.

Daryaee, T. "Mind, Body, and the Cosmos: Chess and Backgammon in Ancient Persia," *Iranian Studies*, vol. 35, no. 4, 2002, pp. 281-312.

Daryaee, "The Ideal King in the Sasanian World: Ardaxšīr ī Pābagān or Xusrō Anōšag-ruwān?," *Nāme-ye Iran-e Bāstān*, vol. 5, 2003, pp. 33-46.

Davis, D. *Shahnameh. The Persian Book of Kings*, Viking, New York, 2006.

Dramiga, J.O. *Eine kurze Kulturgeschichte des Schachspiels*, http://www.schachbund.de/downloads/Kulturgeschichte-des Schachs.pdf, 2009.

Ferdowsī, *The Shahanameh (The Book of Kings)*, Vol. 7, eds. Dj. Khaleghi-Motlagh & A. Khatibi, Bibliotheca Persica, New York, 2007.

Finkel, I. "The World Conqueror Emerges: Backgammon in Persia," in *Asian Games: The Art of Contest*, ed. C. MacKenzie and I.

Finkel, New York, 2004, pp. 88-95.

Franklin, B. "On the Morals of Chess," reprinted in *The Chess Player, Illustrated with Engravings and Diagrams. Containing, Franklin's Essay on the Morals of Chess, Introduction to the Rudiments of Chess, by George Walker, Teacher, to which are added, The Three Games played at one and the same time by Philidor, Sixty Openings, Mates and Situations, by W.S. Kenny, Teacher, with Remarks, Anecdotes, and an Eplanation of the Round Chess Board,* Published by Nathl. Dearborn, Boston, 1841, pp. 7-11.

The History of Łazar P'arpec'i, translated by R.W. Thomson, Scholars Press, Atlanta, 1991.

Ghāsemī, Sh. H. "Peydāyeš-e Šatranj be Ravayat-e Šāhnāme," *Tahghighāt Islamī*, Vol. VI, 1991-1992, pp. 458-466.

Gheiby, B. *Guzāreš-e Šatranj*, Nemudar Publications, Bielefeld, 2001.

Gnoli, G. "Ēr mazdēsn: Zum Begriff Iran und seiner Entstehung im 3. Jahrhundert," in *Transition Periods in Iranian History*, Studia Iranica, Cahier 5, Leuven, 1987, pp. 83-100.

Gnoli, G. Gnoli, *The Idea of Iran*, IsMEO, Rome, 1989.

Grenet, F. *La Geste d'Ardashir fils de Pabag*: Kdrndmg l Ardashir fils de Pdbagd, Die, 2003.

Gunter, A.C. and Jett, P. *Ancient Iranian Metalwork*

in the Arthur M. Sackler Gallery and the Freer Gallery of Art, Smithsonian Institution, Washington, D.C., 1992.

Hansen, O. *Zum mittelpersichen Vičārišn čatrang*, Internationalen Orientalistenkongress in Rom, Verlag J.J. Augustinus in Glückstadt Holst, 1935, pp. 13-19.

Harper, P.O. *The Royal Hunter, Art of the Sasanian Empire*, The Asia Society, New York, 1978.

Herzfeld, E, "Ein Sasanidischer Elefant," *Archäologische Mitteilungen aus Iran*, Vol. III, 1931, pp. 26-28.

Herzfeld, E. *Zoroaster and His World*, Vol. II, Octagon Books, New York, 1974.

Jamasp-Asana, *The Pahlavi Texts Contained in the Codex MK copied in 1322 A.C. by the Scribe Mehr-Âwân Kaí-khûsrû*, Fort Printing Press, Bombay, 1913.

Jamasp Asa, Kh.M. & Navabi, M. *The Pahlavi Codices and Iranian Researches: Manuscript MU2*, eds. Kh.M. Jamasp Asa & M. Navabi, Published by the Asia Institute of Pahlavi University, no. 35, Shiraz, 1976.

JamaspAsa, K.M. and Hintze, A. *The Pahlavi codex MK. Facsimile and Introduction.* Otto Harrassowitz, Wiesbaden, Iranica 20 (forthcoming 2012).

Kellens, J. *Les noms racines de l'Avesta*, Wiesbaden, 1974.

Kennedy, E.S. and van der Waerden, B.L. "The World-Year of the Persians," *Journal of the American Oriental Society*, Vol. 83, 1963, pp. 315-327.

Khaleghi-Motlagh, Dj. "Bozorgmehr-e Bok̲tagān," *Encyclopaedia Iranica*, ed. E. Yarshater, 1989, http://iranica.com/articles/bozorgmehr-e-boktagan.

Khānlarī, P.N. & M. Roshan, M. ed. *Dāstānhāy-e Bīdpāy*, translated by Muḥammad b. Abdallāh al-Bukhārī, Khārazmī Publishers, Tehran, 1369.

Knauth, W. *Das altiranische Füerrstenideal von Xenophon bis Ferdousi*, nach d. antiken u. einheim. Quellen dargest, Franz Steiner, Wiesbaden, 1975.

Lucidi, M. *Il Testo Pahlavico Vičārišni čatrang ud nihišni nēw-artaxšēr*, Scuola Orientale, Universita di Roma, 1935-1936.

Macuch, M. "Pahlavi Literature," *The Literature of Pre-Islamic Iran. Companion Volume I to A History of Persian Literature*, eds. Emmerick, R.E. & Macuch, M., IB Tauris, London, 2009, 116–190.

Marcotte, R.D. "Anīshīrvān and Buzurgmihr - the Just Ruler and the Wise Counselor: Two figures of Persian Traditional Moral Literature," *Rocznik Orientalistyczny*, LI, 2, 1998, pp. 69-90.

Markwart, J. & de Groot, J.J.M. "Das Reich Zābul und der Gott Žūn," *Eduard Sachau-Festschrift*, Berlin, 1915, pp. 248-292.

Mazdapour, K. Introduction to M. Afšārī, *Tāzeh be tāzeh, now be now*, Sokhan Publishers, Tehran, 1384.

Moazami, M. *Wrestling with the Demons of the Pahlavi Widēwdād: Transcription, Translation, and Commentary*, E.J. Brill, 2014.

Menasce, J. de. "Notes Iraniennes," *Journal Asiatique*, 1949, pp. 1-6.

Monchi-Zadeh, D. "Khusrov ī Kavātān ut Rētak, Pahlavi Text, Transcription and Translation," *Monumentum Georg Morgenstierne*, Vol. II, Acta Iranica 22,E.J. Brill, Leiden, 1982, pp. 47-91.

Mujmal at-Tawārīkh wa l-Qiṣaṣ, ed. M.T. Bahār, Tehran, 1334.

Mujmal at-Tawārīkh wa l-Qiṣaṣ, eds. Omidsalar, O. & Afshar, I., Persian Manuscripts in Facsimile No. 1, Tehran, 2001.

Murray, H. J. R. *A History of Chess*, London, Oxford University Press, 1913.

Nafāyis al-fun,n fī 'arāyis al-'uyūn, ed. Mirza Ahmad, Vol. II, Tehran, 1309.

Nāzerī, I.M. *Andarz ī Ōšnar ī Dānā*, Hermand Publishers, Tehran, 1373.

Nezāmī, *The Haft Paikar (The Seven Beauties), Containing the Life and Adventures of King*

Bahrām Gūr, and the Seven Stories Told him by his Seven Queens, translated by C.E. Wilson, Stephen Austin and Sons, London, 1924,http://persian.packhum.org/persian/main?url=pf%3Fauth%3D176%26work%3D002.

Nöldeke, Th. "Persische Studien," *Sitzungsberichte der K. Adademie der Wissenschaften in Wien*, Phil.-hist. Klasse, Vienna, Kl. 126, Abh. 12, 1892, pp. 21-23.

Nöldeke, Th. "Burzōes Einleitung zum Buche Kalila we Dimna," *Schriften der Wissenschaft Ges. in Strassburg*, Vol. 12, 1912.

Nyberg, H.S. *A Manual of Pahlavi*, Otto Harrassowitz, Wiesbaden, 1964.

Nyberg, H.S. *A Manual of Pahlavi*, Otto Harrassowitz, Wiesbaden, 1974.

Orbeli, I.A. & Trever, K. *Šarang. Kniga o šahmatah*, Leningrad, 1936.

Oriān, S. *Motūn-e pahlavī*, National Library of Iran, Tehran, 1371, pp. 152-157, 226-342.

Pagliaro, A. *Il Testo Pahlavico Sul Giuoco degli Scacchi*, in Miscellanea G. Galbiati, Vol. III, Fontes Ambrosiani VIII, Milano, pp. 97-110.

The Pahlavi Codices and Iranian Researches: Manuscript MU2, eds. Kh.M. Jamasp Asa & M. Navabi, Published by the Asia Institute of Pahlavi University, no. 35, Shiraz, 1976.

Panaino, A. "The Two Astrological Reports

of the Karnamag ī Ardaxšīr ī Pabagan (III, 4-7; IV, 6-7)," *Die Sprache*, Zeitschrift für Sprachwissenschaft, Band 36, 1994, pp. 181-198.

Panaino, A. *La novella degli Scacchi e della Tavola Reale*. Un'antica fonte orientale sui due gixochi da tavoliere piuà diffusi nel mondo euroasiatico tra Tardoantico e Medioevo e sulla loro simbologia militare e astrale. Testo pahlavi, traduzione e commento al *Wiz-arišn î Chatrang ud nihišn î new-ardaxšî r* "La spiegazione degli scacchi e la disposizione della tavola reale," Milano, 1999.

Panaino, A. "Haštpāy," *Encyclopaedia Iranica*, ed. E. Yarshater, 2003, http://www.iranica.com/articles/hastpay.

Pingree, D. "Astronomy and Astrology in India and Iran," *Isis, An International Review Devoted to the History of Science and its Cultural Influences*, Vol. 54, Part 2, No. 176, 1963, pp. 229-246.

Qābūsnāme, ed. Q.-H. Yusefi, Scientific and Cultural Publishers, Tehran, 1375.

Reza'ī Bāghbīdī, H. "Vāže Gozīnī dar Asr-e Sāsānī va Ta'sīr ān dar Fārsī-ye Darī," *Nāme-ye Farhangestān*, vol. 5, no.3, 1998[2000], pp. 144-158.

Rosenthal, F. *Gambling in Islam*, E.J. Brill, Leiden, 1975.

Salemann, C. Mittelpersische Studien. Ersets Stük, *Mélanges Asiatiques tirés du Bulletin de* l'Académie Impériale des Sciences de St. Pétersbourg, Tome IX, Livraison 3, 1887, pp. 222-242.

Sanjana, D.P.B. *Ganje shâyagân andarze Atrepât Mârâspandân, Mâdigâne chatrang and Andarze Khusroe Kavâtân. The Original Péhlvi Text, the same Transliterated in Zend Characters and Translated into the Gujrati and English Languages, a Commentary and a Glossary of Selected Words*, Bombay, 1885.

Schädler, U. & Dunn-Vaturi, A.-E. "Board Games in pre-Islamic Persia," *Encyclopaedia Iranica*, ed. E. Yarshater, 2009, http://iranica.com /articles/board-games-in-pre-islamic-persia.

Shaked, Sh. *The Wisdom of the Sasanian Sages*, Mazda Publishers, Costa Mesa, 1979.

Shaked, Sh. "Payman: an Iranian idea in contact with Greek thought and Islam," *Transition periods in Iranian history. Actes du Symposium de Fribourg-en-Brisgau (22-24 mai 1985)*, Studia Iranica. Cahier 5, Paris: Association pour l'Avancement des Etudes Iraniennes, 1987, pp. 217-240.

Shaked, Sh. "Ayādgār ī Wuzurgmihr," *Encyclopaedia Iranica*, E. Yarshater, vol. 3, London, 1987, pp. 127-128.

Shayegan, M.R. "The Evolution of the Concept of xwadāy "God," *Acta Orientalia Academiae Scientiarum Hungaricae*, 51, no. 1-2 (1998): pp. 31-54.

Skilton, A. *A Concise History of Buddhism*, Barnes & Noble, New York, 1994.

Sundermann, "Artēštārān Sālār," *Encyclopaedia Iranica*, ed. E. Yarshater, 1986:

http://www.iranica.com/articles/artestaran-salar-chief-of-the-warriors-a-high-ranking-title-in-sasanian-times-see-artestar-.

Tafazzolī, A. "Ā'īn-nāma," *Encyclopaedia of Iranica*, ed. E. Yarshater, Vol. 1, London, 1985, p. 692.

Taffazolī, A. "Kamar-e Haft Češmeh," *Iranšenāsī*, vol. 27, 1374, pp. 494-499.

Tafazzolī, A. *Tārīkh-e adabiyāt Irān pīš az Islam*, Tehran, 1376.

Tarapore, J.C. *Vijārishn-i chatrang or the Explanation of Chatrang and other Texts, Transliteration and translation into English and Gujarati. The Original Pahlevi Texts. With an Introduction*, Bombay, 1932.

Thieme, P. "Chess and Backgammon (Tric-Trac) in Sanskrit Literature," *Indological Studies in Honor of W. Norman Brown*, ed. E. Bender, New Haven Connecticut, 1962, pp. 204-216, reprint in his *Kleine Schriften*, teil 2, Franz Steiner Verlag Gmbh, Wiesbaden,

1971, pp. 413-425.

Utas, B. & Dabīrsīāqī, M. "Chess," *Encyclopaedia Iranica*, ed. E. Yarshater, 1991: http://www.iranica.com/articles/chess-a-board-game.

Vevaina, Y.S.-D. "'Enumerating the Dēn': Textual Taxonomies, Cosmological Deixis, and Numerological Speculations in Zoroastrianism," *History of Religions* 50/2, 2010, pp. 111-143.

Weber, D. "On Middle Persian aswār 'horseman, rider' in Pahlavi Documents of the 7th Century," *Nāme-ye Iran-e Bāstān*, Nos. 11/12, 2006-2007, pp. 37-44.

West, E.W. "Note on the Catrang-namak," *Journal of the Royal Asiatic Society*, 1898, pp. 389-390.

Wīdēwdād. The Zand î Jaî t Shêda Dât or the Pahlavi Version of the Avesta Vendidâd, ed. D.D.P. Sanjana, Education Society Steam Press, Bombay, 1895.

Wilkinson, C.K. *Chess: East and West, Past and Present, A Selection from the Gustavus A. Pfeiffer Collection*, The Metropolitan Museum of Art, New York, 1968.

Yalom, M. *Birth of the Chess Queen. A History*, HarperCollins Publishers, New York, 2004.

Zakeri, M. *Sāsānid Soldiers in Early Muslim Society. The Origins of 'Ayyārān and Futuwwa,*

Harrassowitz Verlag, Wiesbaden, 1995.

Zakeri, M. *Persian Wisdom in Arab Garb. 'Alī b. 'Ubayda al-Rayḥānī (D. 219/834) and his jawāir al-kilam wa-farā'id al-ḥikam*, Brill, Leiden, Boston, 2007.

Made in the USA
Las Vegas, NV
17 March 2022